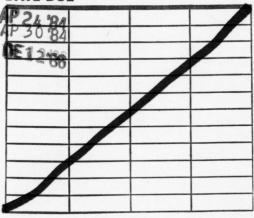

The United States and the Latin American Revolution

Martin C. Needler

University of New Mexico

Allyn and Bacon, Inc.   BOSTON

To Danny

May you have better luck than we did

Printed in the United States of America

Library of Congress Catalog Number: 79-181725

Contents

Preface   **vii**

Introduction   The Problem   **1**

I AN OVERVIEW

1 The Nature of Political Change in Latin America   **6**

*The Roots of Change • The Process of
Political Development • Revolt and Revolution • Revolution by Peaceful Means*

2 The Objectives of Policy   **15**

*The Nineteenth Century • The First Half of
the Twentieth Century • From Eisenhower to
Nixon • Rethinking Policy Goals*

Contents

II SOME DIMENSIONS OF POLICY

3 Communism and Anti-Communism   26

Anti-Communism in U.S. Policy • Should the United States Always Be "Anti-Communist"? • Is Communism a Real Contender for Power in Latin America?

4 The United States and the Latin American Policy   37

The Military "Good Neighbor" Policy • Arms Limitation • Civic Action and Counter-insurgency • The Military as a Modernizing Force • The Military Modernizers in Power

5 The Alliance for Progress   47

6 Recognition of *de Facto* Governments   55

Why Not Automatic Recognition? • Is Non-Recognition Effective?

7 The Implementation of Policy   61

The Style of Policy • Relations with Non-Governmental Organizations and Individuals • Relations with Revolutionary Governments and Publics • Economic Assistance • Military Assistance

III THE RECENT PAST AND THE FUTURE

8 Counterrevolutionary Policies Under Kennedy and Johnson   72

The Invasion of Cuba • The Case of British Guiana • General Policy Approaches Under Kennedy and Johnson • Johnson's Policy on Military Intervention

9 The Dominican Revolution   81

10 Nixon and Latin America   93

11 In Conclusion   **105**

      *National Security ● The Promotion of Demo-
      cratic Government ● Economic Goals*

Selected Bibliography   **114**

APPENDIX: THREE DOCUMENTS

The Charter of Punta del Este   **127**

The Democratic Ideal in Our Policy Toward
Latin America   **145**

Action for Progress for the Americas   **155**

Index   **163**

Preface

In commenting on the manuscript of this book, a distinguished and much respected colleague remarked that it properly belonged to the literature of foreign policy advocacy on Latin America of the late 1950's. It was written, in his view, from the liberal perspective popular at the dawn of the Kennedy era but out of fashion today.

We are all, I think, wiser and more humble than we were when John F. Kennedy took office. Part of our increased wisdom, if that is what it is, has come from the lessons of experience, part from listening to the radical critique of U.S. foreign policy that is the more popular style today.

But the radical and conservative reactions against the liberal idealism of the early 1960's, like most reactions, tend to go too far. The old injunction about babies and bathwater is still apposite. It seems to me that those who still honor the original liberal impulse of the early 1960's should not give up on the problems of policy toward Latin America as insoluble out of bewilderment at the betrayal of the high hopes they had entertained, but should instead shake off the dust of the storm that has passed and see if among the wreckage there are not walls still standing and materials still serviceable for the construction of a new dwelling.

For support during the period in which this book was being written, I would like to thank the Ford Foundation. I am especially grateful to Edwin Lieuwen for his comments and advice. I have also benefited from the characteristically shrewd comments made on a later version of the manuscript by Charles W. Anderson.

Introduction

The Problem

It is no secret that United States policy in Latin America has frequently been highly unsatisfactory, in both conception and execution. To be sure, many of the difficulties that beset U.S. policy could not have been avoided, even by the wisest and most enlightened policy-makers. After all, the United States is large and powerful; the uneasiness and resentment which this fact creates among citizens of weaker countries serve to complicate or obstruct the development of friendly and productive relations, regardless of the substance of U.S. policy. At the same time, Latin America is of course not a homogeneous entity, but consists of states of varying size and interests; and policies that produce satisfactory relations with some states may cause deterioration in relations with other states.

Yet, after the validity of these and similar comments has been acknowledged, it remains true that the history of United States policy in the hemisphere contains far too many acts that were ill-conceived, misinformed, or downright foolish.

The weaknesses of policy are nowhere more apparent than in United States dealings with revolutionary governments. It has often been pointed out that United States policy frequently lacks the merits of traditional diplomacy—its carefulness, tact, and self-control. But even if the United States should master the style of traditional diplomacy, we would still be ill-equipped to meet the problem of conducting relations with revolutionary governments. The merits of traditional diplomacy, great though they be, are more suited to reaching understandings with the aristocratic representatives of status quo governments in the drawing rooms of old Vienna than to furnishing guidelines on how to deal with revolutionary governments.[1]

Realizing the nature of the problem, some commentators and policy-makers have argued that the United States should assume an attitude of sympathy for revolutionary governments, which would enable us to deal with them on a common ground of understanding and friendship. It is certainly true that a sympathetic attitude would go a long way to removing elements of misunderstanding and unnecessary hostility.

But the problem is too subtle and difficult to be resolved simply by a top-level decision to adopt such an attitude, helpful though a decision of this kind would be. The United States is a large and pluralistic country whose influence on other states derives not only from policy decisions taken at the highest level of government, but also from acts of individuals and private corporations; there is not even any assurance that the content of top-level decisions will be reflected in the day-to-day actions of American representatives abroad, so large and unwieldy is our foreign policy bureaucracy. At the same time, it has to be recognized that policy-makers change frequently and that a new foreign policy concept imposed at the highest level may have a life of only a few years.

When the situation is viewed from this perspective, it becomes clear that for a country such as the United States the most effective foreign policies are those which not only make sense in themselves, but which are also in harmony with permanent national interests and with generally held attitudes and values. One cannot simply say, in other words, "Beginning at 9:00 A.M. next Monday morning the United States will sympathize with revolutionary governments." An attempt to come to terms with the reality of the revolutionary movement in Latin America must also come to terms with the reality of American society and character. Within that context, the United States must attempt to develop a tradition of foreign policy which can survive as a basis for effective and productive action but which is at the same time authentically American—a tradition that can become so pervasive and self-evident that the everyday behavior of a second-rate foreign service officer in a minor Central American embassy will reinforce and not undermine the goals of national policy.

The problem, then, is a dual one. On the one hand, we must understand the character of the revolutionary changes that are taking place in Latin America; that is the subject of Chapter 1. On the other hand, we have to

---

[1]This point is stressed by Stanley Hoffman in "The American Style: Our Past and Our Principles," *Foreign Affairs,* 46, 2 (January 1968).

arrive at an understanding of what constitute permanent United States interests and legitimate objectives in our Latin American policies; Chapter 2 will focus on this question through an analysis of the major historical lines of policy. The balance of the book will examine first the character of policy with respect to certain key questions, then where U.S. policy stands currently and what its future orientation should be.

I

An Overview

1

The Nature of the
Latin American Revolution

THE ROOTS OF CHANGE

In Latin America today, a revolution is in progress, a revolution that springs from many causes and has many aspects. Its results are economic, social, and political. While some of its causes are obscure, others can clearly be located in the dimensions of demography and technology.

The rate of population growth in Latin America is higher than that in any other region of the world. This means that there is pressure by the rural population on the limited supply of arable land, while in the cities there is a growing demand for jobs and urban services. The problems of the cities are rendered more acute by a high rate of migration from rural to urban areas.

At the same time, the new generations forming in Latin America are different from their grandparents in expectations and sophistication. This means that the social and economic changes that are taking place are translated into changes on the political scene.

THE PROCESS OF POLITICAL DEVELOPMENT

In Latin America today, a revolution in communications is in progress with the spread of literacy and the ownership of radios, bringing with it heightened awareness of the national community and of political events. At the same time, the colossal movement to the cities that is under way means that the masses are more able to have an impact on politics, since in the Latin American context politics is primarily an urban affair. In societies traditionally structured along rigid lines of class and caste, the idea of human equality is beginning to take hold, so that people increasingly regard themselves as entitled to participate in politics and to expect that public policy reflect their will.

The drive to participation on terms of equality can be manifested in many ways. One of the most obvious has been the increase in the proportion of the population that votes. The rise in those voting since the time of the first World War has been marked in all of the countries of Latin America except for Argentina and Uruguay, which had already reached a high stage of development early in the twentieth century. This heightening of participation is also reflected in the greater willingness of those voting to vote in their own interest, rather than following the guidance of a *patrón*. In Chile before 1960, for example, rural workers typically voted for the Conservative candidates; today they are more likely to vote for the Christian Democrats or the left-wing parties. At the same time, new organizations that represent the interests of the masses are coming into existence and old ones are being expanded and reinvigorated.

Increased mass participation in politics has a revolutionary effect. There is empirical evidence that in Latin America increased participation goes along with greater dissatisfaction with the established system; factors which lead people to participate, such as changes in attitudes and way of life, are also likely to lead them to question the established way of doing things. The evidence also indicates that the newly politicized lower classes vote primarily for the candidate who promises immediate material gratifications, regardless of ideological orientation.[1] This may be a progressive democrat who espouses constructive policies, but may equally well be a demagogue and opportunist of ambiguous ideological identification.

The demands of the newly participant place a strain on the society's capacity to provide services and welfare, especially when population is rising rapidly. Now it is true that to some extent governments are modernizing and improving their capacity to perform their functions through administrative reform, greater effectiveness in tax collections, and improvement in the technical skills of government personnel. Thus in a sense the process of political development can be regarded as a sort of race between the growth of

---

[1] See Daniel Goldrich, "Toward the Comparative Study of Politicization in Latin America," in Dwight Heath and Richard Adams (Eds), *Contemporary Cultures and Societies of Latin America,* New York: Random House, 1965.

participation and the growth of economic and political capacity to meet the demands made by the newly participant.[2]

The key element in determining whether government can keep up with the mobilization of demands, and thus whether it will be possible to maintain the continuity and stability of the political system, is the country's economic capacity. Economic change and growth, which fuel the process of political mobilization, at the same time can provide the wherewithal to meet the demands issuing from that mobilization; in so doing they help to determine the fate of the political system.

If the system proves chronically unable to satisfy the demands of the newly participant masses, thus creating a classic revolutionary situation in which a rising level of expectations is frustrated,[3] then the expression of mass

Table 1   The Increase in Political Participation: Percentage of Total Population Voting in Presidential Elections, Mexico, 1911-1970

Year	Percentage
1911	.13
1917	5.3
1920	8.3
1924	10.4
1928	10.3
1929	12.8
1934	12.8
1940	13.3
1946	10.1
1952	13.3
1958	22.2
1964	22.8
1970	27.6

Source:
Martin C. Needler, *Politics and Society in Mexico*, Albuquerque: University of New Mexico Press, 1971, p. 97.

Note:
Prior to 1917, presidential elections were indirect. In 1958, women voted for the first time in national elections. In 1970, the voting age was lowered to 18.

[2] See Karl W. Deutsch, "Toward an Inventory of Basic Trends and Patterns in Comparative and International Politics," *American Political Science Review*, 54, 1 (March 1960), p. 39.

[3] See James C. Davies, "Toward a Theory of Revolution," *American Sociological Review* (February 1962).

Table 2   The Increase in Political Participation: Percentage of Total Population Voting in Presidential Elections, Chile, 1938-1970

Year	Percentage
1938	9.16
1942	9.15
1946	8.73
1952	15.95
1958	17.90
1964	31.82
1970	30.29

Sources:
a. 1938-1958, *Chile Election Factbook*, Washington, D.C.: Institute for the Comparative Study of Political Systems, September 1963, p. 15.
b. 1964, *The Chilean Presidential Election of September 4, 1964*, Part II, *Ibid.*, 1965, p. 4.
c. 1970, author's calculations based on voting returns reported in the *Diario Las Américas* for September 6, 1970, and population figures given in *Datos Básicos de Población en América Latina, 1970*, Washington, D.C.: Pan American Union, 1970, p. 39.

Note:
In 1952, women voted in national elections for the first time. In 1962, permanent registration was introduced.

demands can begin to take the form of violence. In the initial stages, this violence is not directed to the overthrow of the political system but is instead what might be called "representational" violence. That is, it consists of strikes, street demonstrations, and the like, whose aim is to create a difficult situation for the government, to give new urgency to the demands being posed and enable them to command a higher priority on the government's agenda.[4] In other words, at this stage mass violence may not imply a rejection of the system but rather a desire to participate in it and receive its benefits. \

If representational violence of this type remains without effect, then mass action may develop openly revolutionary aims. However, in the Latin American context, things rarely reach this stage. What typically happens instead is that if a sudden and drastic change resulting in a shift in power to

[4]In several countries of the area, government is so unable to meet popular demands that it is necessary to resort to open violence even to attain such modest goals as the payment of teachers' or government workers' back salaries.

the masses appears possible, then a military seizure of power takes place.
Subsequently, the military government either returns power to conservative
hands after putting down the manifestations of mass violence, or else retains
power, either openly or behind the scenes, in order to repress mass discontent
or to neutralize it by redirecting it against foreign interests.

Thus a period in which political development, in the sense of
heightened participation, is taking place is also likely to be a time of
increasing violence in politics. The political action of the masses becomes
more extensive, more exigent, and more violent, while this in turn causes the
policy of the possessing classes to become more extreme, more violent, and
more repressive. The revolutionary demands of the masses are met by the
"revolutionary" seizure of power by the military.[5]

REVOLT AND REVOLUTION

Of course, the term "revolution" is overused and misused in Latin America,
and a few distinctions about the wide variety of phenomena to which it can
refer should be made. In a general sense, "revolution" means extensive and
fundamental social change, and it is on revolution in this sense that most of
this book focuses. However, the term is commonly applied to any
extra-constitutional change of government, and a great deal of misunderstanding and deliberate misrepresentation of the purposes of political
movements is possible unless one analyzes the concept further.

The traditional "palace revolt," thought of as the typical Latin
American revolution, still occurs, although it has become very much less
frequent in recent years.[6] This is an extra-legal change in officeholders due to
simple personal ambitions, which does not imply major changes in policy, at
least insofar as the economic and social order is concerned. This type of
revolt was more common in an era of limited mass participation when
government was the affair of a limited class and the lives of the masses were
little touched by government. In an era in which mass political mobilization is
taking place, this form of political change occurs less often.

What might be called the "good government" revolt still occurs in Latin
America, as it always has. This is the revolt designed to bring to an end a
government regarded as arbitrary, corrupt, and self-seeking. Thus it involves

[5]See Martin C. Needler, "Political Development and Military Intervention
in Latin America," American Political Science Review, 60, 3 (September
1966).

[6]See Peter Calvert, "The 'Typical Latin-American Revolution'," International Affairs (January 1967).

not only a change in governing personnel but also a change in the way the regime is run. This sort of revolt is generally welcomed by the majority of the population because of the type of government that is removed. Usually, however, it originates within an elite and takes place without mass participation. Lacking social and economic goals, its demands are met with the institution of honest and constitutional rule.

The *"modernizing"* revolution goes beyond these limited goals in having as its objective the restructuring of government, the public service, education, and in general, the established public sector, or the traditional sphere of government action, to make them more efficient and more sensitive to modern techniques and values. There need be very little class content in a revolt of this type, which is often led by a military concerned that national prestige and military efficiency are being impaired by the failure of the traditional rulers to keep up with the times. The revolts common in the late nineteenth century and aimed at the reduction of the powers of the Catholic Church in education, the introduction of civil marriage, and so on, were of a "modernizing" type.

The *"democratizing"* revolution does have class content. It is aimed at reforming traditional political practices, expanding the suffrage, guaranteeing the honesty of elections, and in general at promoting mass participation in politics. Revolts of this kind were common in the early years of the twentieth century, and in many countries their goals have been achieved. But there are still countries of Latin America whose political structures have not been democratized. In Ecuador, for example, only "Ecuadorean citizens" may vote, and only those who can read and write are citizens. The one-third to one-half of the population that is illiterate—principally impoverished Indians—are legally not even citizens of their native country.

The *"socializing"* revolution has as its objective the improvement in the social and economic condition of the masses through a redistribution of national wealth and income. This is increasingly the type of revolt occurring today. It is this type of political change that is most feared by the possessing classes, although the "democratizing" revolt is also feared on the quite correct assumption that if the masses can participate in politics on terms of equality they will soon vote themselves laws that have a socializing tendency.

Revolutions of the types discussed above occur in mixed as well as simple forms, and different objectives are usually held by different leaders within the group making the revolution. In addition, counterrevolutions by those whose interests would be adversely affected may be aimed at forestalling or reversing the tendencies represented in each of the types of revolt described above. Thus, for example, the Brazilian "Revolution" of 1964 was a composite of a "good government" revolt directed against the corruption and unconstitutional tendencies of the government of João

Goulart, plus some "modernizing" intentions, plus a counterrevolution against the democratizing and socializing implications of some of the actions of the Goulart regime.

Awareness of this composite nature of a revolution may make it difficult to take an evaluative position towards it, since one may approve of some of the tendencies it represents and disapprove of others. Given the nature of the general social and economic forces at work in Latin America today, however, particular attention has to be paid to what a revolutionary movement signifies on the democratizing and socializing dimensions.

Because of this composite nature of many revolutions, conflict typically develops, after the success of the revolutionary movement, among elements that collaborated in it, concerned about different objectives, they are brought into conflict by the need to frame and implement a government policy. In a composite rebellion of the 1964 Brazilian type, the ease with which new policies can be obstructed makes it possible for positive goals, such as those of modernization, to be blocked, leaving only the negative goals—those of a counterrevolutionary character—actually achieved.

REVOLUTION BY PEACEFUL MEANS

The term "revolution" is much used in Latin America and, given the fact that many archaic institutions and practices still exist, fundamental structural change is clearly needed to adapt the Latin American societies for life in the modern world. But the achievement of revolution in this sense, revolution *as an end,* does not mean that change can be brought about only by an extended process of violence, by revolutionary *means.* It is possible to have a peaceful revolution; and it is possible to have extended "revolutionary" violence which leads to no change in the status quo at all, as often occurred in nineteenth-century Latin America.

The manner in which basic change can be brought about varies from one country to another, depending on the balance of social forces that exists. In some cases, it seems that extended violence is necessary. In the Dominican Republic before the civil war of 1965, for example, it could be assumed that any serious attempt at social change, or even at honest government, would be undermined and obstructed by the corrupt and brutal warlords who had inherited the command of Trujillo's armed forces.

In most of the Latin American countries, however, the use of violent means may not be necessary to bring about major social change. Violence may even be counter-productive for bringing about desired social change because it starts in motion a process that cannot be controlled and whose end cannot be clearly foreseen, and because it develops patterns of behavior inimical to the rational and civilized conduct of public affairs. Most importantly, in Latin America today the forces of revolutionary change may be the first to take up violent means, but the forces of counterrevolutionary repression, once aroused, can usually master the situation. In that game, "clubs are trumps," as Thomas Hobbes put it. In the typical case it may be wiser and ultimately more effective for the partisans of change to tread softly and not arouse the torpid watchdogs of the status quo.

As the forces of economic and social change have registered their effects on the political situation, the balance of forces has shifted to make possible structural change by evolutionary and even by parliamentary means in several countries. Since the middle of the 1950's, Venezuela seems clearly to have made the transition from an era of the self-interested rule of military autocrats to that of civilian control, constitutional practice, and reformist government. Chile has left behind its traditional situation of social-economic stagnation and has begun a movement toward full political equality and greater social welfare. Slowly and painfully, Colombia is beginning a program of social and economic reconstruction, although the process may be taking place too slowly to be effective. In several countries, in other words, a viable middle ground of constructive evolutionary innovation is being created between the extremes of either last-ditch defense of the status quo or the unleashing of an era of violence in the hope that a better world will somehow come of it.

It is interesting to note that the possibility of structural change without violence exists even in some countries where the balance of political forces does not appear favorable for reform through parliamentary channels. It should be emphasized that these are possibilities only and that they may not become actualities—but they at least make it reasonable to hope. In several countries economic development has begun in areas previously sparsely populated under conditions of greater social equality than the national norm. As migration continues to take place into these development areas from regions of more traditional economic and social structure, after a time the balance of population may shift and the norms that govern national society may come to be provided not by its traditional hierarchic sector but instead by its new more egalitarian sector. Something of the sort seems to have occurred in Venezuela as the center of population shifted from the Andean states to the areas closer to the coast. Today, improved means of transportation have greatly increased personal mobility, and the high rate of movement from rural to urban areas is well known. What needs to be stressed is that movement also occurs from the less developed to the more developed regions, which are at the same time more egalitarian and open.

This appears to be happening currently in Ecuador, where the coastal provinces and especially the city of Guayaquil have experienced a very high rate of population growth, so that now more people live on the coast than in the conservative, quasi-feudal regions of the sierra. Clearly, it needs a generation or two for this process to be consummated and for the national balance of power to shift, but that is also the length of time it takes for a revolutionary government taking power after a civil war to reshape national institutions, after all, *if* the revolution gains power, *if* it is able to maintain itself against internal and external opposition, *if* its leadership is not seduced by the lure of power for its own sake, etc.

Modernization and social development by means of this type of geographic "end run" around the traditional economic and social structures may also be feasible eventually in Bolivia, with the opening up of the Oriente region around Santa Cruz, and in Honduras, with the development of San Pedro Sula and the surrounding coastal region. In Mexico, similarly, the expansion of the more egalitarian societies of the developing areas in the north of the country is helping to offset the high population growth of the traditional Indian regions in the center of the country. In some countries more may be hoped for from conscious government plans to facilitate population movement to developing modern regions than either from efforts to get reform proposals passed by legislatures dominated by conservative economic interests and implemented by an incompetent, corrupt, and ineffective bureaucracy, or from attempts to organize a successful and incorruptible revolution.

There is often little that the United States can or should do to affect the strategies pursued by a country's leadership; often any direct, explicit, or deliberate effort by the United States in that direction would be inappropriate and counter-productive. However, to the extent that United States actions, no matter how circumspect, "low profile," or unobjectionable, are relevant to the choice of alternatives made by national leaderships, it is clear that United States interests lie with the forces of evolutionary change where these are viable, rather than with those of either revolutionary violence or repressive immobility. The extreme alternatives are very costly and in any case generally ineffective. The secular forces at work mean that structural change will come about sooner or later; the task of statesmanship is to try to see that change comes about with a minimum in human costs and a maximum in the realization of human values.

2

The Objectives of Policy

Commonly, foreign policies are justified by reference to a country's "national interests." Yet it is clear that on occasion people want their country's policies to embody certain values or to promote certain ideals whether they advance its *material* interests or not, and even when they impose some material cost. Japanese cars may outsell American cars in Europe, let us say; but most Americans would not therefore think the CIA justified in sabotaging the Toyota factory. National *objectives,* that is, must be conceived of not only as "national interests" in a narrow, purely material sense, but also as embracing ideal aspirations to some extent, and as limited by moral restraints.

Two further criticisms of the way in which the concept of "national interest" is conventionally used in the literature of foreign policy analysis should be noted. One is that typically the appeal to national interest becomes a sort of mystical incantation and no attempt is made to identify specific national interests and to relate specific policies to them in a concrete way.

The other is that very often the conception of national objectives which the writer wishes to urge is not one that "comes naturally" to American policy-makers and diplomats. If it were adopted as a basis for policy, accordingly, it would require a continual effort of will to maintain it, an effort unlikely to outlive a single administration or a single Secretary of State.

It would be going too far, on the other hand, to argue that because there are continuities in national policy that transcend the preferences of individual officeholders, then the foreign policy advocate has no function; that abiding national interests and objectives will inevitably determine that the lines of policy will take certain directions. There is a role for sophisticated advocacy in clarifying objectives, specifying their significance in concrete cases, clearing away factual misunderstandings, pointing out logical and factual inconsistencies. It remains true, however, that a sound national foreign policy which offers a possibility of coherence and continuity must be based on national objectives that grow out of abiding national interests and attitudes. One of the ways of determining what these abiding national interests and attitudes are is to look at the history of policy and attempt to identify how much of the rationale for historical policies remains of relevance today.

THE NINETEENTH CENTURY

From the gaining of independence to the Spanish-American War, the objectives pursued by the United States in its Latin American policies can be grouped under four headings: territorial, economic, ideological, and strategic. In practice, of course, these different orders of objectives are not isolated but impinge on each other, sometimes in mutual support, sometimes in mutual contradiction.

Territorial objectives played a leading role during the nineteenth century, but are no longer of significance. A great deal of military and diplomatic effort was devoted to securing the expansion of the territory of the United States to its present boundaries, by means both fair and foul, at the expense of the indigenous inhabitants, or of Spain and Mexico. By the end of the Spanish-American War, however, this impulse had clearly run its course. The territories acquired as a result of that war—Cuba, the Philippines, and Puerto Rico—demarcated the limit of U.S. territorial expansion; Cuba and the Philippines were later given national independence, and Puerto Rico, although considered "incorporated" into U.S. territory by the courts, remains thus far in an ambiguous status of neither statehood nor independence.[1] Clearly, the present national boundaries of the United States are fixed, and territorial aggrandizement, certainly in the traditional sense of the gaining of territory to be incorporated into the national domain, can no longer be

---

[1] The Panama Canal Zone, a strip of land ten miles wide extending on either side of the Canal, is administered by the United States, but it has never been incorporated into the territory of the United States proper and will undoubtedly revert to Panamanian jurisdiction when arrangements are completed for the construction of a new Canal.

considered one of the objectives of policy. The other traditional economic, ideological, and strategic objectives of policy are not so clearly outmoded, however.

The Monroe Doctrine, announced by President Monroe in 1823, was a statement of policy establishing ideological and strategic objectives for the United States. It signified United States support for the independence of the Latin American republics and opposition to the extension or revival of the colonial systems of the European powers where they had been overthrown in the hemisphere.[2] The Monroe Doctrine was based on considerations both of security and of political principle. Opposition of principle to colonialism as a system complemented the security-based desire not to have to contend with strong and potentially hostile neighbors.

The conception that inter-American relations could be used for promotion of the economic advantage of the United States lay clearly behind the first successful attempt at inter-American organization, the establishment by James G. Blaine of the Commercial Bureau of the American Republics in 1888.

THE FIRST HALF OF THE TWENTIETH CENTURY

It should be noted that in Blaine's approach the national economic advantage was to be served by the promotion of trade. When the pursuit of economic advantage again became a leading motif of United States policy toward Latin America, under the administration of William Howard Taft, its focus had shifted from the promotion of trade to the protection of investment. On occasion, the investments whose protection have come into question under this policy were direct investments—that is, they consisted of enterprises owned and operated by United States companies. During the early twentieth century, however, they were more commonly bonds held by United States citizens, often issued by the government of a small Central American or Caribbean country, on which scheduled payments were not being made. The "Roosevelt Corollary" to the Monroe Doctrine even held the United States to be obliged to insure that payments were made to European bondholders, on the premise that if it did not want European powers to intervene in the

---

[2]It is interesting, though not germane to our present purposes, to note that in fact the policy was not completely followed and there were actually some minor colonizations and recolonizations that took place subsequent to its announcement. See Samuel F. Bemis, *The Latin-American Policy of the United States,* New York: Norton, 1967 (first publication: 1943), pp. 98-105.

Western hemisphere, the United States would have to do their intervening for them.

Thus the national security objectives which, in the original Monroe Doctrine, were linked with the political objective of the promotion of republican forms of government became, in the early twentieth century, linked instead with economic objectives whose stress was on the protection of investment rather than the promotion of trade. In support of this combination of strategic and economic objectives, Presidents Theodore Roosevelt and Taft developed a series of diplomatic, economic, and military techniques: non-recognition of new governments, economic pressures, and the landing of Marines. These techniques, it should be noted, were applied not in South America, which remained in effect the sphere of influence of the British navy, but in the Caribbean region that (despite the language of the Monroe Doctrine and its later interpretations) was the effective United States sphere of influence.

Woodrow Wilson represented a political party less identified with business interests than the Republicans of Taft and Roosevelt. An academic political scientist genuinely committed to the promotion of the practices and values of constitutional democracy, Wilson used the same range of methods employed by Taft and Roosevelt—non-recognition of governments, economic pressures, and military intervention—but with Wilson, as with Monroe, the goals of national security were again linked with the promotion of republican forms of government in the hemisphere. Wilson's policies met with only limited success, and the Republican administrations that followed him tried to draw back from the extreme interventionism that characterized the Wilson years. The goal of the promotion of constitutional democracy that Wilson had stressed was not altogether abandoned, however, and for a time the United States accepted the Tobar Doctrine, embodied in the Central American treaties of 1923, which stipulated that governments coming to power by extra-constitutional means would not receive diplomatic recognition. The more extreme manifestations of U.S. intervention were gradually dismantled and abandoned during the twenties and early thirties, and in 1933 the Roosevelt administration formally accepted the principle of non-intervention in the internal affairs of other states.

Under Roosevelt's Good Neighbor policy the link between the protection of U.S. investment abroad and the national security was broken, and the President resisted pressures to retaliate against Mexico when the government of President Cárdenas expropriated United States oil interests. In providing technical assistance and in promoting trade on terms favorable to the Latin Americans, Roosevelt made economic policy subservient to national security policy, which he understood primarily as the cultivation of friendly relations. The promotion of constitutional democracy as such was not a major objective of Roosevelt's policies, and governments of dubiously democratic credentials were included in the warm embrace of good neighborliness. The main street of Managua was renamed Avenida Franklin D. Roosevelt by the dictator of whom Roosevelt is supposed to have said "He may be an s.o.b., but he's *our* s.o.b." Nevertheless, the ancient truth that governments based on similar political principles tend to sympathize with each other in international relations was rediscovered during World War II, and U.S. recognition was withheld from several new governments whose ideological proclivities suggested that they would sympathize with the Axis powers. Moreover, association with the United States in the war against the fascist powers exerted a democratizing influence, most importantly in the case of Brazil.

President Truman is generally not well regarded in Latin America. Although the concept of U.S. foreign aid, at least in the sense of technical assistance, was made a permanent feature of policy during his term of office, in reality this represented no more than a continuation of programs begun under Roosevelt. Moreover, the needs of postwar reconstruction and the onset of the Cold War with the Soviet Union led the Truman administration to give major attention to Western Europe, to the neglect of Latin America. Attention was paid to Latin America, if at all, only as a Cold War battlefield; that is, the Truman administration began the policy, carried to extremes in the subsequent administration, of regarding movements for revolutionary change in the area as *ipso facto* Communist, of lending support to obnoxious dictators because they were anti-Communist, and of bringing pressures to bear on the Latin American governments to adopt overtly anti-Communist policies in international relations, pressures which were often felt to derogate from national sovereignty and dignity.

FROM EISENHOWER TO NIXON

In the policies of the Eisenhower regime toward Latin America considerations of economic interest, national security, and ideology were fused in an unself-conscious way by Secretary of State John Foster Dulles into a consistent policy of pure anti-Communism. To Dulles, the anti-Communist formula was justified in terms of all three objectives of policy. Communism, or anything that looked to a not-too-discriminating eye to resemble Communism, seemed to Dulles to menace U.S. interests and aspirations in all three dimensions. In the dimension of political ideology, the atheist character of Communism threatened what Dulles took to be the fundamentally religious character of United States political ideals. It might be noted parenthetically that Dulles himself was the son of a Presbyterian minister and

that two of his children became ministers of religion. At the same time, Communist and Socialist governments expropriated private property, which threatened U.S. investors and thus national economic interests. And Communists, however identified, were taken to be necessarily agents of Soviet power and thus members of an international conspiracy against the security of the United States. It would be understating the case to say that Dulles' understanding of the world and of United States interests in Latin America was poor political theory, poor strategy, and poor apprehension of the factual situation.

The Dulles policy reached its maximum expression with the CIA-sponsored invasion of Guatemala in 1954 and open United States support for unsavory dictatorships such as that of Pérez Jiménez in Venezuela. After Dulles' death and the demonstration, in the hostile reception met with by the 1958 mission of Vice-President Nixon to Latin America, of the depths of popular hatred for what United States policies had come to represent, U.S. policy under Dulles' successor, Christian Herter, began to change in the direction that later became embodied in the Alliance for Progress.

The low point reached by United States relations with the Latin American countries during the Eisenhower years laid the basis for the "one minute to midnight" anxieties under whose auspices the Alliance for Progress was born. Under Kennedy, the ideological struggle in which the United States was engaged was reinterpreted as a struggle for democracy rather than simply a negative anti-Communism, and U.S. recognition was withheld from military regimes seizing power from elected governments. Economic relations were to be made subservient to basic political goals by the institution of a massive program of economic assistance. However, the understanding of foreign policy as a vehicle for promotion of private economic interests persisted and found its home, as always, in the Congress; and it wasn't long before the Alliance, which had begun with the objective of promoting economic development in Latin America, became, especially after Kennedy's death, a vehicle for the protection and promotion of private U.S. economic interests.[3]

Kennedy did not actually represent a complete break with the modes of looking at the world of the Eisenhower administration; he was rather a transitional figure. Despite the attempts of the official chroniclers of the Kennedy period, in the aftermath of Dallas, to endow Kennedy with infallibility, the Bay of Pigs fiasco was the natural outgrowth of an anti-Communism on the part of Kennedy of the same character, though doubtless less obsessive, as that which animated Dulles. As the Kennedy

---

[3]For a comprehensive discussion of this point, see Simon G. Hanson, *Dollar Diplomacy in Modern Style*, Washington, D.C.: Inter-American Affairs Press, 1970.

foreign policies became corrupted into those of the Johnson years, the anti-Communist fixation assumed almost the proportions it had had under Eisenhower, as Johnson blundered his way into the Dominican intervention.

As President, Richard Nixon faced the dilemma characteristic of Republican administrations, of having to achieve a reconciliation between fundamentally contrary impulses. Like the Republican administrations of the 1920's, the Nixon administration wished to reduce the costly and far-reaching commitments imposed by the messianism of the previous Democratic administrations. A less interventionist stand on the part of the United States would mean reduced economic aid and military assistance and therefore budgetary savings. At the same time, however, less interventionism would also mean a lessened capacity to protect U.S. investment overseas, almost as much a traditional Republican preoccupation as budget-cutting. It might also mean that the international Communist conspiracy would pick up yardage in the Cold War football game, and it should be remembered that Nixon's anti-Communism, though tempered by time, was of the Dulles vintage.

In subsequent chapters we shall examine in turn the problems of Communism and anti-Communism, U.S. policy toward the Latin American military, the Alliance for Progress, and the recognition of new governments, before returning to a more detailed analysis of the policies of the Kennedy, Johnson, and Nixon years. What we should note here is the persistence, through a variety of different administrations, different historical periods, and different sets of circumstances, of the conception that U.S. policy toward Latin America had to take into account questions of economic interest, national security, and ideological principle, and had to reconcile in some way all three sets of interests and aspirations into a single line of policy.

RETHINKING POLICY GOALS

The task of achieving a reconciliation of these interests into a basis for policy that has relevance and applicability today and tomorrow we shall leave for the concluding chapter. Because of the overriding importance usually ascribed to the goal of national security, and because much of the present malaise about U.S. foreign policy stems from disillusion with the self-defeating lengths to which the country has been carried by a clearly counter-productive conception of the policies mandated by national security interests in Southeast Asia, it is worth examining the objective of national security in detail at this point.

The logical basis of the primacy of national security as a national objective is the assertion that of all the state's objectives, that of its own preservation must have an absolute priority over all others, together with the assumption that the military defense of the state is equivalent to the preservation of its independent existence. However, this fundamental premise is unsound for several reasons.

We should first recognize that the concept of the state, although a useful abstraction, is after all no more than an abstraction, and that it is only under circumstances of total thermonuclear war that the existence of the American *people* ever comes into question; in other areas of national security policy national survival itself is not at stake, and it does not help the rational determination of policy to assume that it is. Accordingly, there is no persuasive case to be made for the absolute primacy of national security interests, conceived in a military sense, over other considerations in our dealings with Latin America. If the premise of absolute priority falls to the ground, then national security considerations must earn the weight to be assigned to them in a general calculation of U.S. interests in any particular situation, by an estimate of the actual consequences that can be expected to flow from different courses of action. In fact, as Arnold Wolfers has pointed out, the level of national security at which countries aim is not given automatically by the logic of the maintenance of the independence of a national state, but is in fact a question of preference, tradition, and the resources that people wish to divert from the attainment of other goals.[4]

Two other characteristic problems about arguments based on national security requirements and strategic considerations should be noted. In the first place, although claims for national security demand the highest priority, they are usually designed to prepare against future contingencies and are thus frequently based on unprovable assumptions about behavior under hypothetical circumstances. In this dramatic and arbitrary world of the imagination it is only to be expected that simple self-assertion and will to power, able to pose as the highest patriotism, should come into their own.

This sort of effect seems clearly to have been present in the policies of Theodore Roosevelt, for example. The explicit preoccupation with problems of national security that led to the assertion of U.S. military power in Panama and the Caribbean seems in reality to have been less the actual prompter of his policy orientation than the desire to cut a heroic figure that appears to have animated all of Roosevelt's behavior, personal as well as public.

In the second place, what are usually presented as national security concerns deal only with what Samuel P. Huntington once called "negative" national security, that is, the attempt to prevent loss. Typically overlooked in such calculations is "positive" national security, ways in which the nation's security can be augmented by positive acts. A policy of supporting

---

[4]Arnold Wolfers, "National Security as an Ambiguous Symbol," *Political Science Quarterly,* 67, 4 (December 1952).

dictatorships *à la* Dulles, for example, is designed to prevent other people, who may have hostile attitudes to the United States, from coming to power—at least in the short run. Of course at the same time, by identifying the United States with unpopular governments, it itself contributes to creating those hostile attitudes. A policy of positive national security, on the other hand, might instead be directed at creating favorable rather than hostile attitudes, to the extent possible, among people who are going to come to power sooner or later anyway.

At this point, the promotion of national security joins hands with ideological concerns. Aspirations for democracy, human dignity, and welfare which characterize the political ideas of North Americans are shared by South Americans too. There need be no "necessity for choice" on this point. North Americans can enjoy the luxury of having national policy reflect ideological aspirations and, by so doing, create a community of aspiration with the peoples of Latin America that in fact heightens national security. This was the secret of the success of the Latin American policies of Franklin D. Roosevelt, in which there was not the contradiction between a progressive and pro-democratic posture and the requirements of national security in time of war that showed itself to some extent in his domestic policies. The point was made explicitly in the Rockefeller Report:

> Practically, nations with broadly based political systems of a democratic type are more likely to have outlooks and concepts compatible with the style of the United States and its people, and more willing to cooperate with us in establishing an effective world order.
>
> All Americans, in fact, share a common heritage of respect for human dignity, justice, and freedom of the individual.[5]

---

[5] *The Rockefeller Report on the Americas,* Chicago: Quadrangle Books, 1969, p. 57.

II

Some Dimensions of Policy

3

Communism and Anti-Communism

In many ways, the United States was extremely unfortunate in the manner by which her induction as a major participant in world politics came about. In the nineteenth century the United States field of action in international relations was the northern part of the Western hemisphere. Remaining true to the tradition of Washington and Monroe, the United States abstained from involvement in the politics of Western Europe. Her foreign policy was essentially one of local predominance or local imperialism, as exemplified by the westward movement. Wars were fought against the Indians, against Mexico, and finally against Spain, to establish American hegemony in the northern part of the hemisphere. This task was completed before the outbreak of World War I, and annexationist sentiment was spent with the acquisition of Puerto Rico.

Despite the subsequent interventions in Central America and the Caribbean, no political movement arose thereafter urging the annexation of these territories to the United States, as had occurred in similar situations during the nineteenth century. That is, the establishment of the national boundaries appeared definitive and the policy of local predominance had run its course. At the same time, the growth of American economic and military power made it clear that the United States would be called on to play a role in world politics and not simply in the local politics of the immediate surrounding area. The war with Spain marked a transition here; the war began in the Caribbean but was extended across the Pacific, and it did, after all, involve the defeat of a Western European power. However, the United States was still not clearly ready to assume the role of a world power until it intervened in World War I. Even then, traditional sentiment for holding aloof from the quarrels of Europe was strong enough to delay United States entry and to lead to a resurgence of traditional hemispheric isolationism after the war. But the balance had been shifted by the intervention in World War I, and from then on the United States was irretrievably an actor on the stage of world politics.

Psychologists say that the patterns initially learned for any new set of behavior, especially when reinforced, tend to determine behavior thereafter. The United States first became committed to participation in world politics in order to wage war against an imperialist power, Wilhelmian Germany. Yet typically, a nation newly participant in international politics, lacking a foreign policy tradition and still unsure about where its genuine national interests lie in cases in which it is not directly concerned, tends to decide its position on the basis of ideological principle.[1]

In order to rationalize United States participation in the war to himself and to his countrymen, Woodrow Wilson cast it in terms of an ideological struggle for democracy.

Whatever doubts there may have been about this formulation of the problem in the case of World War I, it clearly applied with great force to the situation that occasioned United States re-entry into the arena of world politics after the isolationist period with participation on the Allied side in World War II. Thus the understanding of American participation in world politics as a fight for democracy against an antidemocratic imperialist power was reinforced by the experience of the struggle against Hitler.

The situation which followed the war seemed again to fit into the same pattern, and the manner in which the situation was conceived, and the response it engendered, came almost by reflex. Again, an imperial power—this time the Soviet Union—was attempting to impose an anti-democratic system on the world and again the United States was called to take up arms in the name of defending a democracy that was identified with American interests and the American way of life.

At the same time, some dissident voices were raised which attempted to interpret the situation in a different light. Thus it was argued, for example, that the Soviet Union only *talked* as though it planned to extend its system

---

[1]See the discussion of ideologism in Herbert J. Spiro, *Government by Constitution,* New York: Random House, 1959, pp. 195-196.

everywhere, but that in reality the primary Soviet concern was local hegemony in Eastern Europe or even simply defense of national borders. Probably the most reasonable interpretation of Soviet intentions is that they were indeterminate. They doubtless began with the defense of the borders of the Soviet Union; they could not realistically aim at world hegemony in any foreseeable future; but between those limits it was likely that Stalin intended to augment national power and influence wherever this could be done without excessive cost.[2]

Yet in developing its response to the new situation that had emerged, a response that was designed, arguably but not unreasonably, to meet the maximum possible threat, the United States made the key error of identifying the threat to American interests and values not as Soviet ambitions but as Communism. The power of the psychological forces that went into appraising the situation in this way, and in magnifying the extent of the threat, can be seen by the fact that the doctrinal form given United States policy did not change even though it was very soon demonstrated that any threat that existed came from Soviet ambitions and not from Communism *per se*. The clearest demonstration of this point came with Tito's breakaway from Soviet dictation, which began in 1947. Thereafter it should have been realized that a state could be Communist and yet need pose no threat to the United States—it could in fact be an ally of the United States and pose a threat to the Soviet Union itself. Yet the United States accepted the thesis that Stalin desperately and implausibly tried to maintain, that only those who unquestioningly obeyed his dictates were "real" Communists; others who called themselves Communists were really something else; "Communism" meant, in effect, subservience to the Soviet policy line.

The misapprehension of the situation that United States policy-makers had fallen into was carried one step further: Communism was perceived as the single overriding threat to United States values and interests. The rigidly blind approach to international politics that developed in the United States thereafter led to absurd, self-contradictory, and self-destructive conclusions. Three armchair followers of Marx in a minor Central American or Caribbean country suddenly became a threat to the United States. The gangster-president who banked the results of his thefts in Switzerland while torturing and massacring his subjects became an honored friend of the United States because there were Communists among those he massacred. Some of the most

---

[2]Of course, this is a much controverted question: For an extended discussion, see Martin C. Needler, *Understanding Foreign Policy,* New York: Holt, Rinehart and Winston, 1966, pp. 102-107; see also Arthur M. Schlesinger, Jr., "Origins of the Cold War," *Foreign Affairs,* **46,**1 (October 1967), p. 36, and Harold Macmillan, "The World Today," *Political Science Quarterly,* vol. 83, no. 1 (March 1968), p. 7 *et. seq.*

shameful episodes in all of United States history resulted from this willful misapprehension of the situation.

As a result of the attempt by Secretary Dulles to appease Senator Joseph R. McCarthy by allowing the latter's standards to become those of State Department personnel policy, the foreign service officers who survived the McCarthy era, if not themselves witch hunters, were frequently either witless or spineless. The pall cast over the integrity and courage of foreign service officers during that period has not been completely lifted in the succeeding years.

One of the most flagrant and direct ways in which McCarthyite attitudes continue to do damage to United States interests in Latin America, for example, is in the granting of visas to visit the United States. Time and again, distinguished and influential Latin American leaders have been refused permission to visit the United States, often in an insulting and humiliating fashion, because some frightened junior consular official was afraid that a liberal or radical association in the applicant's background could be used against the official to damage his career prospects in a future anti-Communist witch hunt. This incredible practice, by which the United States almost systematically converts its potential friends into its enemies, continues today.[3] If any rationale exists for this policy at all, it is presumably the assumption that anyone with Communist associations is necessarily *ipso facto* a Soviet espionage agent. Although many unsophisticated Americans still believe this to be the case, it is of course not so.

SHOULD THE UNITED STATES ALWAYS BE "ANTI-COMMUNIST"?

The crowning irony in this whole question of the United States' attitude to Communism, however, has now been provided by the evolution of the tendencies within Communism, or more exactly perhaps by our deepened understanding of those tendencies, which has taken place in recent years. As it has become clear, with the development of tendencies within Communism more radical than that represented by the Soviet Union, that Communism is not monolithic, it has at the same time become clear that the so-called Moscow line is itself not invariably inimical to the interests of the United States. Thus in the realm of inter-state relations, the United States has found it in its interest to collaborate with the Soviet Union in matters relating to

---

[3]For the detailed discussion of specific cases, the reader is referred to Marian Wilhelm, "Cárdenas—Friend into Foe," *Christian Science Monitor,* (June 12, 1961); and Frank Tannenbaum, "Castro and Social Change," *Political Science Quarterly* (June 1962).

arms control and the avoidance of war through accident or miscalculation, in attempts to keep violence from breaking out or spreading so as to involve the two super powers in a confrontation with each other, and in checking the expansion of a third power to which both are unfriendly. As the conception of common Soviet and American interests develops, cooperation in other areas is coming to appear of mutual advantage, even where traditional rigidities mean that such collaboration must be implicit only. It has been noted, for example, that in one Asian country in which both the United States and the Soviet Union have aid programs, stretches of a road built separately under the two countries' auspices somehow manage to meet and turn out to be of the same width.

In the domestic politics of Latin America, the time is approaching for the United States to acknowledge that the policies of the moderate Moscow-line Communists can be complementary to the policies of the moderate left and progressive center. This means that there is no *a priori* reason for the United States to take alarm, say, at the victory of a presidential candidate backed by the Moscow-line Communist Party.

The moderating effect on the left of the traditional Communist Parties can be seen in a variety of circumstances. The Venezuelan Communist Party, for example, has explicitly and repeatedly condemned attempts to overthrow governments of the moderate left by violent means and has conducted a running propaganda battle with Fidel Castro.

In Mexico the leading representative of the moderate Moscow-line approach until his recent death was Vicente Lombardo Toledano, the leader of the Popular Socialist Party, rather than the ineffectual Dionisio Encina, the general secretary of Mexico's Communist Party[4]; Lombardo's analyses of Mexico's political situation were always impeccably Marxist, and yet they did not prevent him from collaborating steadily with the government Party of Revolutionary Institutions, of moderate center-left orientation. Lombardo's reasoning, which is also that of the traditional Communists in most countries of Latin America, ran as follows. Socialism is a higher stage of human development than capitalism. Therefore socialism cannot be constructed until capitalism has attained its maximum development and collapsed of its own contradictions. The Latin American countries, however, are just emerging from the feudal stage and embarking on the construction of capitalism. Therefore in order to prepare the way for the future construction of socialism, it is the duty of activists of Marxist orientation to collaborate with the national bourgeoisie in order to bring an end to the remnants of feudalism and make possible the construction of a capitalist system. Only then will the

---

[4] See Karl Schmitt, *Communism in Mexico,* Austin: University of Texas Press, 1965, *passim.*

development of a proletarian class provide a basis for the emergence of a strong socialist movement. In the meantime, Marxist leadership of workers' movements should be educational in the sense of developing a socialist consciousness among the workers and in teaching techniques and habits of organization. Thus there are no objections to collaborating with the moderate center and center-left in the present era of history. Eventually, of course, the forces of the proletariat and those of the bourgeoisie will clash when the development of capitalism has run its course. But that day is a long way off and in the meantime a policy of collaboration is in order.

The "soft" Moscow line even extends to foreign capital. The Soviet publication *New Times* of July 19, 1967, argued "In the present situation, the newly independent countries can benefit by making use of foreign capital, provided . . . that (it) is placed under strict local control and the overall economic interests of the given country are safeguarded."[5]

It is precisely because of this moderate orientation of the Moscow-line Communists that the revolutionaries of the New Left hold them in such scorn and contempt. Nevertheless, because of it the traditional Communist parties in Latin America today usually present no threat to the evolution of the Latin American societies and economies toward modernization. And, of course, to someone who is not committed to the Marxist view of history, there is no inevitability about the succession of socialism to capitalism, so that in effect the traditional Communists are lending their efforts to the construction of a modern society and economy on the basis of a quite false assumption that they will be heirs of that society. But that is their worry, not ours.

What this means in practice is that the United States should be ready to appraise political situations as they actually are and not let doctrinaire preconceptions distort perceptions of reality.

If it is true that democratic forces of the moderate left can engage in limited cooperation with traditional Communist parties, it is equally true that there are other Communist and socialist tendencies with which cooperation is not possible. Each case has to be evaluated carefully and realistically on its merits. The point is that it is no longer adequate to apply the label "Communist," which then brings automatically with it a series of consequences for U.S. policy actions.

The question of members of Communist parties' sharing in government power, for example, is difficult. The critical question here is whether under such circumstances they would be prepared to operate within the established

---

[5] Quoted in Elizabeth K. Valkenier, "New Trends in Soviet Economic Relations with the Third World," *World Politics,* 22, 3 (April 1970), p. 429.

framework of constitutional practice and policy. In other words, would Communist members of a government respect civil liberties, hold free elections, and leave office if defeated? Would a government under Communist leadership conduct its international relations on the same basis as other Western hemisphere governments, or would it regard itself as committed by ideology to a foreign policy of automatic hostility to the United States and automatic following of the Soviet policy lead? The answers to these questions are not yet clear—probably not in the minds of Latin American Communist leaders themselves; and for most countries the question will remain moot for a long time. If the experience of Eastern Europe is any guide, however, it appears that Communist governments can be kept subordinate to Moscow only if the threat, and on occasion the reality, of intervention by the Red Army is constantly present—which would not be true in Latin America.

Thus many Americans who thought in traditional terms took fright when the government of Salvador Allende in Chile, while not Communist-led, took office in 1970 with Communist participation. But although Allende's relations with the United States could not be called friendly, they were correct, and he made clear that his government would respect the country's constitutional and legal framework.

Lest the reader think that it is quite unlikely that a Communist-led government could bind itself to operate within a framework of constitutional government and friendly relations with the United States, it is worth pointing out that such a case did in fact exist and the United States, after hesitating, did not apply the criteria proposed here but instead those of automatic anti-Communism. The case was that of the government of Cheddi Jagan in what was then British Guiana (now Guyana). Jagan was himself a Marxist, although the party he led was not ideologically committed. He headed a legally elected and constituted government which posed no international threat to its neighbors or to the United States. Jagan applied for aid from the United States under the Alliance for Progress program, indicating his agreement with its objectives and undertaking to respect constitutional liberties in Guyana. After at first granting the request, the Kennedy administration changed its mind and delayed fulfillment, eventually collaborating covertly in an attempt to overthrow Jagan. British military forces finally intervened to remove him from office and during the subsequent period of control from London the electoral law was changed to work to the disadvantage of Jagan's party, which lost the subsequent election. As it happens, the resulting government, headed by Forbes Burnham, is considerably more cavalier with civil liberties and constitutional procedures than Jagan's government was. If Jagan should return to power, and again request that his government receive aid from the United States—for he appears to be an incurable optimist—what would Washington's reaction be?

IS COMMUNISM A REAL CONTENDER FOR POWER
IN LATIN AMERICA?

Despite the fact that the rhetoric of United States relations with Latin America has been filled for two decades with phrases about the "Communist menace," in fact this supposed threat is very minor indeed, where it exists at all. But the possessing classes in Latin America, and especially the armies of the area, have taken up the anti-Communist theme with even greater enthusiasm than shown in the United States. In fact, there is a wave of creole McCarthyism currently under way in Latin America, comparable to that experienced by the United States during the 1950's. The "loss" of Cuba stands in the same relation to this Latin American McCarthyism as the "loss" of China stood to the United States variety. It has promoted confusion, a search for scapegoats, and an essentially paranoid approach to politics.

The coming to power in Cuba of a government that refers to itself as Communist has, ironically, been misunderstood by those on the revolutionary left just as much as it has been by Latin American conservatives. These misapprehensions of both extremes have fed on each other, and have combined to produce an image of the political conflict in Latin America as that between revolutionary dictatorship and last-ditch defense of the status quo by any means as the only alternative courses of action. To the revolutionary leftists, liberals and moderate progressives of the center are deluded tools of "the establishment," while to the fanatics of the right wing they are allies or dupes of the Communists. The United States would be extremely ill-advised to accept this distorted view of the political situation. There are many viable paths of action lying at neither extreme, and vital forces between the extremes do exist and are capable of framing and implementing constructive programs.

Thus, for example, there was no inevitability in the evolution of the Cuban Revolution to the point where it became identified with Communist doctrine and style of government. The fact of the matter seems to be that the identification of the revolution as Communist was not compelled by any inner necessity but was instead the result of an essentially arbitrary act on the part of Fidel Castro.[6] This is clearly demonstrated by the fact that many who fought with Fidel Castro in the mountains in fact saw the situation quite differently, believing there to be other constructive paths for the revolution to follow, and have been imprisoned, executed, or forced into exile by the Castro government.

---

[6]This appears to be the conclusion of most academic commentators. See, for example, Peter Calvert, "The Typical Latin American Revolution," *International Affairs*, **43**, 1 (January 1967).

The Soviet Union has never completely accepted the Castro government in Cuba as authentically Communist in their sense, and indeed Castro has followed the lead of the Soviet Union in international relations only irregularly. It is fairly clear, in fact, that in many ways the Soviet Union is quite unhappy about the evolution of the Cuban regime. The Cubans' economic bungling[7] has meant that the Soviet Union has to support the Cuban economy at a cost of over one million dollars a day, while Castroite heresies have introduced another element of discord into a Communist camp already split several ways. Soviet defense of Cuba has also caused unpleasant and humiliating confrontations with United States military power, and the failure of Khrushchev's "adventurist" policy in Cuba was one of the reasons cited for his removal from office. It is an open question, therefore, whether the Soviet Union could afford another Cuba, either economically or politically.

However, it is not likely that the Soviet Union will indeed be faced with another Castro in Latin America, who, by volunteering to join the Communist camp, can impose an onerous financial and political burden. Certainly the Moscow-line Communist Parties in the various Latin American countries oppose any attempts to mount revolutionary efforts of the *fidelista* type. In criticizing such attempts on tactical grounds they are undoubtedly right, as the failure of Che Guevara's pathetic attempt to turn the Andes into the Sierra Maestra of South Amemica demonstrates. The totally un-Marxist rationale developed by Régis Debray for the Guevara movement indicates in fact the bankruptcy of the Guevara approach to revolution. In Debray's thesis, the insurrectionary band itself constitutes the nucleus of the revolutionary movement and of the future post-revolutionary state. In effect, however, this constitutes an acknowledgement that under the circumstances of present-day Latin America there is in Marxist terms no revolutionary class. The rebel army has to become the revolutionary movement since there are no revolutionary possibilities either in the proletariat of classic Marxist analysis or in Mao Tse-tung's peasantry.

Under some circumstances the normally conservative and apolitical peasantry may become a revolutionary force—at least until land has been seized, after which the peasants revert to their normal conservative

---

[7]The extent of this is so incredible that one must cite Cuban Revolutionary sources so as not to be accused of hostile exaggeration. Major Guevara, as usual, made up in frankness what he lacked in skill as an economist. See "The Cuban Economy," *International Affairs*, **40**, 4 (October 1964), reprinted in John Gerassi (Ed.), *Venceremos: The Speeches and Writings of Che Guevara*, New York: Macmillan, 1968, especially pp. 353-355. More recently, the economic failings of the Revolution were discussed by Fidel Castro himself, in his speech of July 26, 1970. The full text of the speech can be found in *The New York Review of Books* (September 24, 1970).

orientation—but this is true only under unusual circumstances, which are difficult to create deliberately. Organized labor in Latin America, although the classic revolutionary class of Marxist analysis, is in fact a quite unrevolutionary elite enjoying a particularly favored and protected situation under Latin American circumstances, the laws governing hours of work, wages, and social security giving it in fact a privileged position.[8]

A rapidly growing population element in Latin America which appears at first glance to have revolutionary potential is clearly next on the list for discovery by Marxist theoreticians of revolution. This is the urban poor, whose shantytowns have mushroomed on the marginal lands of Latin American cities, following on the population growth and accelerated movement to urban areas of the last twenty years. There has been discussion of the revolutionary potential of this element by non-Marxist observers for some time, and recently the Brazilian Carlos Marighela has begun to be recognized posthumously as a theorist of "urban guerrilla warfare," occupying a position analogous to Che Guevara's as the theorist of the rural guerrilla.

The dweller in the urban shantytown, however, like the peasant, may have revolutionary potential, but only under certain circumstances. A fair summation of our present state of knowledge would probably be that the dwellers in the shantytowns can become active participants in serious revolutionary violence only after open fighting has already broken out and is under way.[9] Normally, politics has little salience for the shantytown dweller and normally he is too absorbed in the struggle for existence to take an active part. Moreover, many shantytown dwellers think of their situation as improving and have hope for the future, which means that their revolutionary potential is limited.[10]

In their analysis of the current situation in Latin America, in other words, it appears that Lombardo Toledano and the Moscow-line Communists are essentially correct. There is a revolution to be made in Latin America, but it is a bourgeois revolution. Feudal survivals are strong, indeed are still dominant in some countries, economies are still largely dependent on

---

[8]See Henry Landsberger, "The Labor Elite: Is it Revolutionary?" in Seymour Martin Lipset and Aldo Solari (Eds.), *Elites in Latin America,* New York: Oxford University Press, 1966.

[9]See José A. Moreno, *Sociological Aspects of the Dominican Revolution,* Cornell University Latin American Studies doctoral dissertation series, Ithaca, New York, 1967, p. 133.

[10]See Wayne A. Cornelius, Jr., "Urbanization as an Agent in Latin American Political Instability: The Case of Mexico," *American Political Science Review* (September 1969); and Gino Germani, "La Ciudad como Mecanismo Integrador," *Revista Mexicana de Sociología* (July-September 1967).

agricultural products, and the framework of a modern society and govern-ment is still to be established. Under these circumstances, the coming to power of a Communist government is more likely to be the result of a combination of unforeseeable circumstances, as in the case of Cuba, than the result of some deliberate plan growing out of a body of sophisticated doctrine.

Communists may participate in governments without leading them, as in the Allende government in Chile, however. But the case of Allende shows that these may be governments with which the United States can coexist perfectly well. Governments may come to power irreconcilably hostile to the United States and determined to do it damage. But such governments need not be Communist, and governments with Communist participation need not fall into that category. United States policy should be to avoid having irreconcilably hostile governments come to power, using the means discussed in the previous chapter. But this is not the same as defining the enemy as "Communism" and acting accordingly.

4

The United States and
the Latin American Military

THE MILITARY "GOOD NEIGHBOR" POLICY

Despite the general skepticism of most Americans about the political role of
the military services of the Latin American countries, the United States
maintains good official relations with Latin American military officers. These
good relations, especially those between United States officers attached in
various capacities to embassies in the Latin American countries and their local
colleagues, are usually regarded with some suspicion by Latin American
civilians. When a *coup d'état* occurs, for example, the United States military
attaché is often suspected of conniving in it, even when it is known that the
ambassador himself was opposed. Some Latin American commentators have
even gone to the extent of speaking of one policy followed by the State
Department and AID and another followed by the Pentagon and the CIA. It
is at least true that alert ambassadors take special pains to ensure that their
service attachés represent their policies accurately to their Latin American
counterparts.

It clearly makes good practical sense for the United States to attempt
to maintain good relations with Latin American military officers; they are
usually an important political force and may at some future time be in key
government positions. Accordingly, the conscious attempt is made to have all
Latin American officers of field grade (major and above) spend some time in

the United States either taking training courses or on short orientation visits, if they have not previously visited this country. Of course, the political purposes involved can hardly be stated in so many words, and the close relations of military personnel across national boundaries are normally justified in ways other than announcing that the intention is to augment U.S. political influence.

Until recently, the fiction was maintained that international military cooperation was necessary for collaboration in the defense of the hemisphere against outside attack. This position was of course argued during the Second World War, but it was also revived in the era of the Cold War. Nevertheless, it is an open secret that no effective Latin American contribution to the defense of the Western hemisphere can reasonably be expected. Thus, for example, toward the end of the Eisenhower administration the hemispheric defense thesis culminated in joint military maneuvers of the United States and the armed forces of five countries of Latin America. Analyzing the exercises, Hanson Baldwin, the military correspondent of the *New York Times*, wrote, on March 11, 1960:

> Despite the excellent performance of the Latin American participants, the maneuvers emphasized what was already known: that United States forces must continue to shoulder the major military burden in the Western Hemisphere. Latin American nations have virtually no strategic capability; that is, the capability of transporting or projecting their military strength to other parts of the hemisphere by sea or air transport.

Good military relations were also maintained through a program of subsidized arms sales, and in some cases outright free gifts of arms. The rationale for this program was that it was necessary for all Western hemisphere forces to use the same weapons in order to simplify logistic problems in the event of the joint defense effort that was the premise of military cooperation.

Although the military forces of Latin America went along with the doctrines of hemispheric security, their actual concerns were not these but rather problems of internal security and defense against their immediate neighbors. Thus Argentina was concerned not with the military threat from Russia or China, but with that from Brazil or Chile. Peruvian armed forces watched carefully the armaments levels not of the Warsaw Pact countries but of Chile and Ecuador.

Concern over the possibility of military threats from their immediate neighbors was as realistic, or unrealistic, for the Latin American military as it was for the military of countries elsewhere. Some wars have been fought in South America in the twentieth century, and in Central America border incidents, exile invasions, and military expeditions are quite frequent. It is clear nevertheless that major wars between hemisphere countries today are unlikely, while the maintenance of a high level of military preparedness does impose a burden on the weak economies of the area—though not, it should be noted, a burden greater than those borne by countries in other regions of the world. (In fact the percentage of gross national product devoted to military spending in Latin America is lower than in any other region.[1])

ARMS LIMITATION

Perhaps in recognition of the economic burden of military preparedness, initiatives for arms control have been made by conservative politicians representing established national economic interests. Jorge Alessandri, President of Chile between 1958 and 1964, made strenuous efforts to secure agreement on arms limitation during 1959 and 1960, but without success. Manuel Prado, also a representative of business interests, who was President of Peru during approximately the same period, was likewise a strong advocate of arms limitation.

Clearly, arms limitation can only come about through mutual agreement, since no state wishes to put itself at a disadvantage relative to its neighbors. However, the problem of securing agreement is made particularly difficult by the checkerboard pattern of military rivalries in South America. That is, Argentina tries to match its force and arms levels with those of Brazil; but any increase in Argentine military capabilities provokes uneasiness in Chile. Yet the attempt by Chile to match an Argentine arms buildup induces the Peruvians to augment their own military strength, which in turn causes uneasiness in Ecuador. Thus a bilateral agreement to limit arms levels or arms purchases would in most cases not be enough in itself to avoid competitive arms buildups. It is axiomatic, however, that an agreement is more difficult to reach the greater the number of states that are involved. This is especially true in the Latin American case, because of the frequency with which governments change and the high order of military influence on those governments. Nevertheless, it is in the direction of multilateral agreement that the solution to the problem of unnecessary expenditures on arms lies, and the United States should do everything feasible to facilitate the negotiation of such a multilateral agreement.

Failing such an agreement, it is entirely inappropriate for the United States to attempt unilaterally to hold down the level of armaments in any one

---

[1]See United States Arms Control and Disarmament Agency, *World Military Expenditures, 1966-67,* Washington, D. C.: Government Printing Office, 1968, p. 9.

Latin American country, although this has been tried intermittently, the most recent case being the attempt early in 1968 to prevent the Peruvians from acquiring supersonic jet fighters. Such an effort is quite unseemly, besides being ineffectual. In making the attempt, the United States is in effect arrogating to itself the right of determining what are the legitimate defense needs of another country, which is not only unreasonable but a direct derogation of the sovereignty of the other country. This sort of thing comes with particularly bad grace from the United States, which maintains a fantastically high level of military capabilities designed to meet every conceivable, and sometimes even barely conceivable, hypothetical military situation. The bad grace of such an action is compounded by the fact that the United States itself is a major producer and supplier to other nations of costly

Table 1   U.S. Military Assistance to Latin America, Fiscal 1953-1966
(In Millions of Dollars)

Argentina	87.6
Bolivia	17.6
Brazil	374.1
Chile	143.4
Colombia	102.3
Costa Rica	2.0
Cuba[1]	16.1
Dominican Republic	19.6
Ecuador	52.9
El Salvador	5.3
Guatemala	13.4
Haiti[2]	4.5
Honduras	6.1
Mexico	6.7
Nicaragua	9.4
Panama	2.3
Paraguay	8.3
Peru	134.3
Uruguay	44.5
Venezuela	66.8
Regional	18.6
TOTAL	1,135.8

[1] No assistance since 1961.
[2] No assistance since 1963.

Source:
Study on "The Latin American Military" prepared for the U.S. Senate Subcommittee on American Republics Affairs by Edwin C. Lieuwen, Washington, D.C.: Government Printing Office (October 9, 1967), p. 36.

Table 2   Size of U.S. Military Missions in Latin America, as of December 31, 1966

Country	Officers	Enlisted	Civilian	Total
Argentina	33	26	2	61
Bolivia	26	22	2	50
Brazil	53	54	12	119
Chile	23	21	1	45
Colombia	34	29	1	64
Costa Rica	3	7		10
Dominican Republic	27	15		42
Ecuador	31	34		65
El Salvador	11	9		20
Guatemala	13	12		25
Honduras	10	10		20
Nicaragua	7	12		19
Panama	2	2		4
Paraguay	12	10		22
Peru	32	33	1	66
Uruguay	15	13	1	29
Venezuela	36	40		76
TOTAL	368	349	20	737

Source: Lieuwen, op. cit.

weapons, and so attempts to keep sophisticated and expensive arms out of the hands of Latin Americans usually seems to them resentment at the arms' having been ordered from European suppliers rather than the United States.

It appears likely that the anti-United States posture of the Peruvian officers who seized power later the same year grew in part out of resentment over the action of the United States in attempting to deny Peru supersonic jets.

But in any case unilateral action of this type seems bound to be ineffectual, since so long as the country in question believes there to be a need for the arms it will try to get them, and there are always arms suppliers that the United States cannot control. When the United States tries to bring pressure on its allies not to sell arms to a Latin American country, which then goes on to buy them from France or Czechoslovakia, the only effect is to penalize cooperative allies, which lose the sale.[2]

What is important in affecting the political predispositions and role of the Latin American military is not the question of whether or not they

[2]For a thoughtful discussion of the arms sales question, with special reference to the Peruvian case, see Luigi Einaudi, *Peruvian Military Relations with the United States*, Santa Monica, Calif.: RAND Corporation, 1970, especially pp. 42-45.

receive arms from the United States on favorable terms. There seems no evidence that military aid programs have had an effect one way or another on the political role played by Latin American armies.[3] If United States policies have encouraged military intervention in politics, it has been by the concept embodied in the counterinsurgency and civic action doctrines developed by the United States during the 1960's and enthusiastically adopted by the Latin American military that armies have an important role to play in development, together with the extreme anti-Communist position encouraged by the United States. It is the height of naïveté to argue, as Governor Rockefeller did in his report to President Nixon, that the United States had contributed to a more democratic orientation among Latin American military officers through "the exposure to the fundamental achievements of the U.S. way of life that many of the military from the other American countries have received through the military training programs which the U.S. conducts in Panama and the United States."[4] Latin American military officers do not display democratic orientations; and the influence imparted by their contacts with the U.S. military has not been in a democratic direction.

In fact, the influence is more frequently the other way. As Senator Frank Church once put it, often ". . . American military officers located in these countries come to espouse and to parrot the viewpoints of the local military people."[5]

CIVIC ACTION AND COUNTERINSURGENCY

Although the armed forces of the Latin American countries covet supersonic jets, from the point of view of United States military doctrine during the 1960's what they should instead want are bulldozers and helicopters. With the abandonment of the "hemisphere defense" conception of the function of the Latin American military, there was substituted for it the view that the appropriate functions of the Latin American military were civic action and counterinsurgency. The thesis runs as follows. The real danger to the national security of the Latin American nations today comes from internal insurrections and guerrilla warfare. These should be combated by counterinsurgency

---

[3]See Charles Wolf, Jr., *United States Policy and the Third World,* Boston: Little, Brown, 1967, pp. 109-111.

[4]*The Rockefeller Report on the Americas,* Chicago: Quadrangle Books, 1969, p. 33.

[5]"United States Military Policies and Programs in Latin America." Hearings before the U.S. Senate Subcommittee on Western Hemisphere Affairs, June 24 and July 8, 1969. Washington, D.C.: Government Printing Office, 1969, p. 82.

tactics on one hand and, on the other, an attempt by the military forces to gain popular support, especially among the peasantry, so that the guerrilla will have to function in a hostile environment. The military are to gain the support of the peasantry by operating various programs of immediate social and economic benefit, such as the construction of roads and schools, and aid in agriculture and health. This type of effort is known as civic action. An additional rationale for it that has been advanced is that since there are going to be armed forces disposing of a large share of the national budget in any case, then they might as well contribute to the country's development efforts.[6]

THE MILITARY AS A MODERNIZING FORCE

Some commentators have seized on this latter point and have elaborated it into a general theory that the military can play a modernizing role in Latin America. The military are a modernizing force, the argument goes, since the requirements of military organization and the operation of modern weapons necessarily make them technologically advanced and concerned to introduce the latest methods. Their concern with national strength and prestige, moreover, is believed to give them a wholehearted commitment to modernization, since this will increase the effectiveness with which the nation can act as a factor in international politics. At the same time, their training in a spirit of national service makes them more patriotic and more able to view problems from the perspective of the national interest than are class and sectional elites, who are thought to be concerned primarily with the welfare of their own groups.

This conception of the political orientation and functions of the military owes more to the experience of the Near East and Southeast Asia than it does to that of Latin America.[7] Nevertheless, it has been urged by several commentators on Latin America and has served to promote a more favorable attitude in United States circles toward the military there than has traditionally existed. The traditional conception of the Latin American military was rather that of an incompetent and disorderly group concerned primarily with self-aggrandizement, bent on gaining power and riches by any means, and serving to hold back the development of society not only toward democracy but even to any higher level of civilization.

---

[6]The leading treatment of the genesis and evolution of this doctrine is Willard F. Barber and C. Neale Ronning, *Internal Security and Military Power: Counterinsurgency and Civic Action in Latin America,* Columbus: Ohio State University Press, 1966.

[7]One of the first to develop the thesis of the modernizing military was Lucian Pye, who has worked primarily on Burma and China.

It is certainly true that there have been changes in the military forces and that today it is more likely that a military officer has some technical training and regards himself as committed to the values of patriotism and modernization. However, it would be entirely incorrect and quite dysfunctional for the purposes of United States policy to accept the Latin American military officer's subjective conception of himself as a modernizing patriot as an accurate indicator of his political behavior. Latin American military officers are certainly patriotic. However, patriotism for them means in the first instance the defense of that institution which makes possible the preservation of national independence and autonomy—in other words, the army. Thus the first patriotic duty is to resist all attempts to weaken the army by denying it funds, by attempting to put it under closer control by civilian political authorities, or by creating a militia. Any attempt in this direction is typically regarded as simply the first step in a plan to destroy the military in order to prepare the way for a Communist assumption of power.[8]

Since Fidel Castro followed his seizure of power by disbanding the former army and even shooting some officers, any weakening of the power and autonomy of the army has become synonymous with "Communism" in military eyes, and "Communism" signifies loss of status and employment and possible death.

This tendency of the military to see Red at every opportunity is of course well known in Latin America and is exploited by conservative forces attempting to resist reformist trends. Time and again in recent years conservative economic interests have played on military fears of bloody revolution and the destruction of the armed forces *a la cubana* in order to induce military seizures of power and prevent reformist governments either from coming to power or else from putting through their programs.[9]

THE MILITARY MODERNIZERS IN POWER

Once the armed forces have seized power, then quite frequently they do attempt to act on their desire for modernization. However, modernization under military auspices very often threatens vested economic interests just as much as a social reform program conducted by an elected government, and

---

[8]Even the Chilean armed forces have thought along these lines, according to *Ercilla* of May 18, 1960 (cited in Miles Wolpin, "Chile's Left: Structural Factors Inhibiting an Electoral Victory in 1970" *Journal of Developing Areas,* 3, 2 (January 1969).

[9]See Edwin Lieuwen, *Generals Vs. Presidents: Neo-Militarism in Latin America,* New York: Praeger, 1964.

accordingly the erstwhile conservative civilian partners of the military in staging the seizure of power then turn against the military government and try to undermine it.

Usually, this is not a difficult task. Other civilian political forces are generally ready to put aside old differences and join in an all-party civilian front to oppose military government. The students are always ready to defy the military government's ban on demonstrations and take to the streets. The military rulers, blundering hopelessly in a world of political and economic decisions they do not understand, interpret the student manifestations as a challenge to authority that must be put down by force. As the conflict between mounting repression and mounting resistance escalates, the previously favorable or apathetic population becomes increasingly outraged over the brutality of military repression, and the military government is soon confronted by a totally hostile population. Thus the same newspapers that greeted with joy the accession to power of Castello Branco in Brazil finally come to the opinion that his government represented "a black chapter in Brazilian history."[10] Those who made fun of President Illia in Argentina and applauded General Onganía's seizure of power soon long to be back in the good old days with Illia. The members of the military *junta* that overthrew President Arosemena of Ecuador to general popular acclaim become so hated that they have to take asylum in foreign embassies to avoid being lynched.

In the typical case, the would-be progressive military regime faced, as it tries to govern, by a series of external dilemmas and internal tensions, ends its life as anything but progressive or modernizing. The Brazilian regime that took power with such fanfare in 1965 became, within a few years, a purposeless dictatorship whose brutality was without precedent in Brazilian experience, notorious for having made torture a system of government. General Onganía wandered from one economic policy to another, unwavering only in his determination to use force against labor unions, and was finally removed in 1970 by the same colleagues who had placed him in power four years before. Or the regime can become, like the government of General Torrijos in Panama, the vehicle for the personal rule of yet another of the "strongmen" whose names grace the pages of histories of Latin America. It is clear that, if one has to generalize about the Latin American military as a whole, one must consider their role, on balance, still to be a conservative or reactionary one.

From time to time, it is true, a modernizing military regime manages to surmount the host of problems that await it and remain, at least for a time,

---

[10]Dispatch from Paul L. Montgomery in Brasilia, *New York Times* (March 16, 1966).

faithful to its original progressive impulse. But the existence of such cases no more constitutes an argument in favor of military regimes as such than the occasional appearance of a competent and benevolent monarch argues for monarchy as a system of government. The whole point of the principles of democratic rule and constitutional restraints, evolved so painfully through centuries of human history, is to free men from dependence on the personal characteristics that rulers happen to have and give them assurance of at least a tolerable government no matter how incompetent, self-interested, or ill-willed the governors prove to be. Latin American and North American partisans of the "progressive military regime"—and there are altogether too many of them—are wagering against the odds in betting on the emergence of non-responsible governments that will somehow be dependably enlightened, competent, and careful of human rights.

5

The Alliance for Progress

With the accession of Richard Nixon to the presidency, the Alliance for Progress ceased in effect to be an operating part of U.S. foreign policy and passed into history, although indeed it is questionable as to how integral a part of U.S. policy it was under Lyndon Johnson. There are fashions and fads in commentary on U.S. policy, and the current fashion is to scoff at the Alliance, alleging that it did not succeed in its objectives and that indeed it could not succeed in them. Before we accept this view, however, it is worth taking a closer look at the Alliance to see what of value can be learned from our experience with it.

The formulation and announcement of the Alliance for Progress was part of the reaction to the sense that, under Eisenhower, United States policy in the hemisphere had drifted from crisis to crisis without any clear design or consciously held objectives. The key elements in President Kennedy's formulation of the Alliance, for our purposes, were the following.

First, it clearly established economic development not only as the goal of the United States in Latin America, but also as the presumed goal of the Latin American governments themselves. At the same time, implicit in the theory on which the Alliance was based was the premise that political development, understood in a democratic sense, would accompany or follow economic development.

Second, the Alliance, as it was formalized in the Charter of Punta del Este,[1] set a number of very specific goals which the countries of Latin America were to reach in the process of development. The best known of these was probably the goal of a 2½ percent annual increase in per capita gross national product.

Third, the Alliance embodied a definite political orientation, that is, a distinctive line on questions of public policy. This could be characterized as reformist—rather than reactionary or revolutionary—in the sense that the objective was change, but that this change should be brought about within the existing constitutional and legal framework. There was a self-conscious contrast here with what were assumed to be the views of significant groups in Latin America: the conservative or reactionary views of the upper-class oligarchs, who were assumed to want no change; and the revolutionary views of the supporters of Fidel Castro, or perhaps "the Communists," who wanted change but were prepared to violate norms of constitutional behavior, property rights, and legal freedoms in order to bring change about.

Fourth, the program was to be financed from various sources—domestic savings within the Latin American countries, foreign public funds—but the government of the United States committed itself to providing at least half of all funds needed, which were estimated at $2 billion a year over a ten-year period.[2]

As the end of this ten-year period approached, the mood on the United States side was one of disillusion with the program. Such disillusion had various roots—one of them surely being the general public antipathy to foreign involvements that followed on the unsuccessful Vietnam adventure—but in support of this disillusion various items of evidence could be cited. First, many of the specific goals listed at Punta del Este had clearly not been reached. Second, the political goals of the Alliance had apparently not been reached either. In 1961 there had been only four dictatorships among the twenty Latin American governments; by 1971, there were ten or eleven. Third, U.S. funds had clearly been diverted to purposes not in the spirit of the developmentalist emphasis of the Alliance, such as to help a country out of a balance of payments crisis, or simply to support normal government budgetary expenses. Fourth, there did not seem to be any upsurge in Latin American support for the United States growing out of gratitude for the U.S. funds contributed to the Alliance. In fact, the end of the 1960's was a period

---

[1] The complete text is given as an appendix to this book, pp. 127-143.

[2] This was the informal understanding. Because of the constitutional requirement that appropriations be voted by Congress annually, the Charter of Punta del Este pledged a billion dollars in U.S. aid just for the first year of the program.

of growing economic nationalism of a general anti-Yankee orientation in Latin America.

This mood of disillusionment appeared to receive further substantive support with the publication in 1969 of a detailed study on U.S. aid to one Latin American country, Colombia, prepared by the staff of the Senate Foreign Relations Committee,[3] that reached generally pessimistic conclusions as to the effectiveness of American aid in promoting Colombian development. The report had a substantial impact, especially outside the handful of well-informed observers of the Colombian scene who noted that four of the six years covered by the report were spent under the notoriously "do-nothing" presidency of Guillermo León Valencia, at a time when Colombia's exports were facing a decline in world prices; and that in a longer perspective, the growth of the Colombian economy has actually been quite encouraging, whether or not this was due primarily to the efforts of Alliance programs.[4]

Nevertheless, in the popular consciousness the impression has grown that the Alliance has been an economic failure. The following comment is not atypical:

> In one of his foreign aid messages to Congress, President Kennedy observed that in view of its rate of population growth Latin America would have to double its income over the next thirty years *merely to stand still.* Unfortunately, since WWII (*sic*) most Latin American nations (read underdeveloped nations) have been going the other way. Their incomes have been declining. Needless to say, the result is that the economies of such countries daily grow more stagnant.[5]

---

[3]*Survey of the Alliance for Progress: Colombia—A Case History of U.S. Aid,* Washington, D.C.: Government Printing Office (February 1, 1969).

[4]According to one evaluation of the performance of the Colombian economy made at the end of 1969, "By purely economic criteria, this record could hardly be faulted." *Latin America* newsletter (London), **III** no. 52 (December 26, 1969), p. 413. According to the same source, "Non-traditional" exports (i.e., other than petroleum and coffee) had risen from $90 million in 1966 to $200 million in 1969, while the servicing of external debt took only 13% of foreign exchange earnings. The rate of economic growth had gone from 4.2% in 1967 to 5.8% in 1968 and 7.0% in 1969. Official Colombian government publications, however, gave the GNP growth figures as 6.1% for 1968 and 6.5% for 1969, though estimating the 1970 figure at 7.0%. The improvement over the average 4.7% for 1961-67 was still marked. *Colombia Today* (newsletter of Colombia Information Service), **V**, 8 (August 1970).

[5]"A New Vocabulary for the New Left: Some Reflections on U.S.-Underdeveloped-Area Relations," *Journal of Contemporary Revolution,* San Francisco State College, **I**, 1 (June 1967). Emphasis in original.

As it happens, this statement is erroneous. In sixteen out of twenty Latin American countries, income has in fact grown faster than population, thus making possible an improvement in per capita levels. The special character of the four exceptional cases is worth noting. In Uruguay, per capita national income has indeed deteriorated, but the country is not experiencing the population explosion that is affecting the rest of Latin America, and in any case enjoys a standard of living which is quite comfortable and one of the highest in the region. One does not need to worry, in other words, about starvation and suffering in Uruguay.

There are three other countries whose per capita national incomes have shown stagnation or decline over the last decade: Haiti, Cuba, and the Dominican Republic; but in each case, political rather than economic factors were primarily responsible. The Dominican Republic's economy was set back several years as a result of the civil war and U.S. military intervention of

Table 1   Annual Growth Rates in Gross Domestic Product
                  at Factor Cost, 1960-1969

	Total	Per Capita
Argentina	3.5	1.9
Bolivia	5.4	3.0
Brazil	5.5	2.6
Chile	4.5	2.0
Colombia	5.0	1.5
Costa Rica	7.0	3.1
Cuba	—	—
Dominican Republic	3.4	0.1
Ecuador	4.5	1.1
El Salvador	5.6	2.3
Guatemala	5.2	2.2
Haiti	1.5	-0.8
Honduras	5.3	1.8
Mexico	6.9	3.3
Nicaragua	6.3	3.2
Panama	7.7	4.3
Paraguay	4.5	1.1
Peru	5.1	2.0
Uruguay	0.6	-0.6
Venezuela	4.7	1.3
Latin America	5.2	2.2

Source:
Correo Informativo de la Sociedad Interamericana de Plani-
ficación IV, 13 (April-May-June 1970), p. 6., based on ECLA
figures.

1965. And the poor performance of the dictatorships of Cuba and Haiti can in any case not constitute a criticism of the Alliance, since they do not participate in it.

Actually, a better case can be made that the economies of the Latin American countries are growing satisfactorily. Mexico, Peru, and the countries of Gran Colombia (Venezuela, Colombia, Ecuador) have experienced steady growth since the end of World War II. Brazil's growth has been substantial though not consistent. Since the beginning of the Alliance for Progress, Chile, Paraguay, and even Bolivia have registered respectable, and the Central American countries spectacular, growth rates.[6]

A more sophisticated evaluation of the economic effects of the Alliance for Progress, however, cannot conclude that the Alliance has been a clear failure or a clear success. Some of the specific goals set for the Alliance have in fact been reached. For example, six of the eighteen Latin American countries participating in the Alliance (that is, excluding Haiti and Cuba) have exceeded the goal of a 2.5 percent annual increase in gross national product per capita, despite the rapid rate of population growth. Industrial growth and diversification have been marked, there have been substantial gains in productivity for some crops, and agreements are in effect stabilizing export prices for sugar, tin, and coffee. Life expectancy at birth increased by about four years between 1960 and 1970,[7] just under the five years envisaged in the statement of Alliance goals, and potable water has been made available to over 70 percent of the urban population of the area, exceeding the Alliance goal somewhat.[8]

On the whole range of specific economic and social targets set up at Punta del Este, a fair conclusion would be that some, but probably a minority, have been reached; in almost all respects there has been progress, even where this fell short of the targets. But the targets were after all marks to be aimed at, and not holy writ. Whether equivalent progress would have been made without the Alliance was necessarily a hypothetical question.

Many Alliance goals are clearly of a long-range nature, and it will not be possible to reach a definitive judgment on success and failure with respect to them for some time. We are used to suspending judgment on the

---

[6] The situation through 1964 is discussed in Pan American Union (Department of Economic Affairs), *Latin America: Problems and Perspectives of Economic Development, 1963-64,* Baltimore: Johns Hopkins University Press, 1966.

[7] *Datos Basicos de Poblacion en América Latina,* Washington, D.C.: Organization of American States, 1970, p. 5.

[8] Agency for International Development, *A Review of Alliance for Progress Goals,* Washington, D.C.: Government Printing Office, March 1969, pp. 39-40. Figures on GNP growth are given on p. 13 of the same publication.

achievements of revolutionary governments for an initial period of grace, after all. Thus although Mexico's economic development today seems exemplary, it was twenty-five to thirty-five years after the Revolution of 1910 before economic indicators showed improvement over their pre-Revolutionary counterparts. It took fifteen years before the Bolivian Revolution of 1952 led to any measurable economic improvement, and the Cuban economy is still floundering more than ten years after Fidel Castro marched into Havana.

But most American critics of the Alliance do not seem prepared to think in terms of time periods of this magnitude, although it might be assumed that change which proceeds using only evolutionary means will take longer to take effect than change that uses revolutionary techniques. What can one make, for example, of the plaintive aside of the Foreign Relations Committee report on Colombia that "The country's social structure remains essentially unchanged,"[9] (after all of six years!) when one recalls that the change in social structure referred to entails a complete social revolution?

It should also be noted that some of the goals of the Alliance appear not to have been realized, not because of the faults of the Alliance program itself, but because of the intrusion of extraneous factors, both economic and political, that undermined its efforts. Thus, for example, the progress of the Alliance has been held back because the United States Congress, speaking for various special interests, attempted to have the Alliance serve purposes extraneous to its primary goals and even in conflict with them. A prime example here was the requirement for "additionality"—that is, the requirement that United States funds be used to purchase goods in the United States over and above those normally purchased here, even when those goods cost more than the same items elsewhere, and even when a Latin American country has a surplus of blocked funds in its exchange account with another country that could supply the goods. Happily, this requirement was eliminated by the Nixon administration.

Finally, a considerable burden was placed on the Alliance by the administrative machinery that was established by the United States to manage it, partly to be able to show Congress that the funds provided had not been misappropriated in some way. The criticisms that could be cited under this heading are many. The program was over-administered on the United States side, leading to unnecessary delays and an excessive absorption of available funds by the stipends of United States personnel. President Kennedy's determination to begin the program immediately at its maximum level of spending was unfortunate in that a large sudden expansion in the aid bureaucracy was necessary, which led to a lowering of personnel standards.

[9]*Op. cit.*, p. 3.

At the same time, the governments of several of the Latin American countries paid insufficient attention to the selection and design of projects to be financed.

Probably too much criticism of the Alliance has been directed at the Latin Americans, alleging that they have not been pulling their own weight in the joint effort envisaged at Punta del Este. According to calculations of the Inter-American Committee on the Alliance for Progress, however, 88 percent of total investments made in Latin America during the first seven years of the Alliance was generated internally within the Latin American countries. Moreover, the so-called "aid" of the United States consisted largely of loans rather than grants, and during the first seven years of the Alliance principal and interest payments made by the Latin American countries to the United States equalled slightly over half of the total "aid" provided during the period.[10]

The present mood in commentary, the tendency to say that the Alliance for Progress has been a failure, probably represents a natural and inevitable swing of the emotional pendulum in the sense that it constitutes a reaction to the exaggerated hopes with which the Alliance was inaugurated. It was of course quite naive, although typically American, to believe that simply by injecting large enough amounts of money it would be possible within ten years to reconstruct completely twenty national societies beset by a variety of major economic, social, and political problems. Even revolutionary governments prepared to use violent means need one or two generations to put through such changes--and they don't expect per capita income and welfare to rise steadily during the period in which major structural changes are being made.

The overly mechanical character of this "engineering" approach to the Alliance for Progress is symbolized by the exaggerated importance usually attached to the specific numerical goals of the Alliance, the 70 percent of city dwellers who are to have drinkable water, the 2½ percent annual increase in per capita GNP, which are often regarded as magic numbers representing absolute success or total failure. In social change of the magnitude and scope involved in the Alliance for Progress, there is really no room for concepts of pure success or pure failure; the realistic alternatives are rather improvement on the one hand and deterioration on the other, with all questions ones of degree.

It is also quite consistent with what we know about social and economic change to take the view that improvement is likely to be uneven, with the circumstances of some countries enabling them to move ahead faster

---

[10]Speech to the Inter-American Press Association by Carlos Sanz de Santamaría, Buenos Aires, October 15, 1968.

than others, with periods of only marginal improvement suddenly followed by "breakthroughs," with disorder and turbulence preludes to stability and growth. The attempt to derive measurements based on assumptions of steady, consistent, and visible improvement is thus bound to be unsatisfying and inconclusive in the short run.

This is not to say, as some have argued, that the promise of the Alliance was "oversold" to Latin Americans in its early days. It seems in retrospect that the most important merit of the Alliance was indeed that it did change the mood of public policy in Latin America; it established development as a norm of public policy, as not only a proper concern of government but even its first duty.[11] It should be realized that this in itself constitutes something of a revolution; it is especially important in the Latin American context, where governments change rapidly and sometimes a government comes to power with no clear conception of what its policy aims should be. The strong cues provided by the Alliance for Progress program have, to a large extent, been responsible for reorienting government policy throughout Latin America.

Obviously, social and economic change take a long time to bring about. The first step in bringing them about is to reorient objectives, policy norms, and government priorities. With the Alliance for Progress, this step was taken. It was an important one.

---

[11]This point was also made by Galo Plaza, the Secretary General of the Organization of American States, in a speech in February 1969. See *Survey of International Development,* 6, 3 (March 15, 1969), p. 4.

6

Recognition of *de Facto* Governments

A question that arises repeatedly in the course of United States relations with the countries of Latin America is whether or not to recognize a government that has come to power by extra-constitutional means. The frequency with which governments are overthrown by military *coups* and the inconsistency of U.S. policy on this question have led to a variety of different policies' being adopted, none of which has thus far proved completely satisfactory.

Whether or not a government is recognized by the United States can have a substantial impact, especially in the smaller countries; it affects the government's ability to secure foreign aid and commercial credit, and it can also serve to stimulate or discourage attempts to overthrow the government. These deleterious effects of non-recognition, it should be noted, are economic and political rather than legal.[1]

WHY NOT AUTOMATIC RECOGNITION?

In the search for a serviceable and consistent policy, the attempt has been made from time to time to revive the original U.S. policy on recognition,

---

[1] See John G. Hervey, *The Legal Effects of Recognition in International Law,* doctoral dissertation, University of Pennsylvania, 1928; and Philip M. Brown, "The Legal Effects of Recognition," *American Journal of International Law* (October 1950).

which was adopted when Jefferson was Washington's Secretary of State. Framed originally by Jefferson to deal with the case of the new Revolutionary regime in France, this doctrine established the criterion that a government would be recognized if it was in exercise of actual administrative control (*de facto* control) over the territory of the state, with the question of the "legitimacy" of its title to office not being taken into consideration. The simplicity and self-evidence of this criterion has recommended it throughout the history of United States foreign policy. It is worth noting, however, that except for the first half of the nineteenth century, when foreign relations were not a major concern of the United States government, the criterion of *de facto* control has never been followed for very long.

The lack of viability of the simple *de facto* criterion has been obscured by the fact that it was not simply abandoned but instead gradually modified until it had lost its original meaning. Thus, for example, C. Neale Ronning, in his discussion of recognition policy, opposes a traditional "American Doctrine" on recognition to a "Doctrine of Legitimacy," and writes that the American Doctrine "calls for the recognition of governments whenever they fulfill certain fairly objective requirements—*de facto* control of the State and ability (sometimes 'willingness' is added) to discharge international obligations."[2]

But this doctrine, as stated by Ronning—and this is not an unusual way of summarizing it—is no longer a straightforward *de facto* policy. *Ability* to meet international obligations can be regarded as an aspect of *de facto* control; *willingness* to meet such obligations, however, is a political criterion, the application of which means that recognition policy has become a political tool. Historically, the "willingness" criterion seems deliberately to have been introduced to acquire leverage for the attainment of policy objectives; thus it was used to withhold recognition from new governments in the Dominican Republic until they had accepted the 1900 convention giving the United States control of the Dominican customs.[3] And in fact even the criterion of "ability to meet international obligations" was introduced by Secretary of State William Evarts to give the United States similar bargaining leverage at the time of the accession to office of Porfirio Díaz in Mexico in 1877.

A simple *de facto* policy has proved not viable even for Presidents and Secretaries of State who started their terms of office determined to try to maintain a policy of *de facto* recognition. Thus, for example, Franklin D. Roosevelt and his Secretary of State, Cordell Hull, made it clear that under

---

[2]C. Neale Ronning, *Law and Politics in Inter-American Diplomacy*, New York: Wiley, 1963, pp. 6-7.

[3]William A. Neumann, Jr., *Recognition of Governments in the Americas*, Washington, D.C.: Foundation for Foreign Affairs, 1947, Chap. 2.

the Good Neighbor policy non-recognition would not be used as a political weapon against a Latin American government. Nevertheless, in 1936 and 1937 the United States joined with the other powers that had mediated in the Chaco War between Bolivia and Paraguay in refusing to recognize new governments coming to power in the two states until they had agreed to abide by the settlement of the war that had been made.[4] And of course during the period of World War II, the Roosevelt administration refused to recognize many European governments which did have *de facto* control, while recognizing governments in exile that had no semblance of effective authority, depending on which side they were on in the conflict.

A similar practice developed during the Cold War. In April 1946, Secretary of State James F. Byrnes announced that thereafter the United States would recognize all governments in *de facto* control.[5] However, just seven months later the United States mission was recalled from Albania,[6] and the policy of recognition of all *de facto* governments was subsequently abandoned.

The reason why the United States has not been able to maintain a policy of recognition of all *de facto* governments is quite clear. If there is some value to a government in being recognized by the United States, then recognition becomes a source of leverage, one of the tools in the diplomat's kit, to be used rather than to be thrown away by a policy of automatic recognition. Moreover, if it is not possible to maintain an invariable policy of automatic recognition, and if recognition and non-recognition are used for political purposes, even if only occasionally, then a political decision must be made in *every* recognition case. That is, it is not credible to maintain that new governments in countries A, B, and C were automatically recognized without the United States passing judgment on them, when at the same time the government of country X is not being recognized for political reasons, because the United States does not approve of the government's existence or some aspect of its policy. Once automatic recognition can no longer be applied in every case—and the history of U.S. foreign policy since 1860 seems to indicate that it cannot—then there is no logical alternative to a political recognition policy which makes necessary evaluation of each government whose recognition is in question.

An appreciation of this fact should not be disturbing. It simply means that recognition, like other acts of a government in its foreign relations, is affected by political considerations, rather than being in some kind of legal limbo by itself. In fact, on closer examination, it is even open to question

---

[4]*Ibid.,* Chap. 5.

[5]*Ibid.*

[6]State Department Bulletin (August 31, 1947).

whether the classic policy of *de facto* recognition was really politically neutral, as is usually assumed, or whether it was not itself prompted by political considerations. When Jefferson framed the criterion of *de facto* control, it was the case that most governments in the world were monarchic and what gave a government legitimacy was the principle of dynastic succession. Accordingly, republican governments necessarily had to come to power through extra-constitutional means. Thus to adopt a policy of *de facto* recognition meant in effect to take the side of republican governments, that is, governments based on similar principles to those of the United States and therefore likely to be sympathetic to the United States.[7] Thus in all probability there have always been political implications in this supposedly politically neutral policy.

This does not have to mean that the United States should refuse to recognize any government it dislikes mildly. There should be some substantial reason that will justify the inconveniences and estrangement that go with non-recognition. However, in the cases of many governments such reasons exist, rooted in the security, economic, and ideological objectives of policy.

IS NON-RECOGNITION EFFECTIVE?

An argument commonly used against the political use of recognition, and especially against a conditional threat not to recognize, is that it is an ineffectual weapon of policy and its use therefore makes U.S. policy as a whole appear ineffectual. In support of this argument, it is possible to cite cases in which the United States threatened not to recognize a new government coming to power by force, but the existing government was overthrown anyway.

Although plausible, this objection overlooks several factors. In the first place, if examples of ineffectiveness can be cited, examples of effectiveness also exist. Thus, to pick a couple of instances that come to mind at random, the withholding of recognition forced changes in the cabinet of President Villarroel in Bolivia in 1944, and the threat to withhold recognition[8] probably saved the government of Juan Bosch on several occasions, although Bosch was eventually overthrown.[9] Of course it is not possible, in the nature

---

[7] See Charles Evans Hughes, *Our Relations to the Nations of the Western Hemisphere,* Princeton, N.J.: Princeton University Press, 1928, p. 38.

[8] Known in the Kennedy Administration as "the Loeb formula," since it was first developed for use by Ambassador James Loeb, facing the probability of a *coup* in Peru.

[9] See John Bartlow Martin, *Overtaken by Events,* Garden City, N.Y.: Doubleday, 1968, *passim.*

of things, to enumerate the *coups* that did *not* take place because of a stated policy of non-recognition by the United States of governments seizing power extra-constitutionally, but what we know of the dynamics of the formation of conspiracies to stage *coups d'état* suggests that they consist of fragile coalitions which may fail due to some mild disincentive to one or two people.[10] Thus even if a stated non-recognition policy does not swing the view of the whole officer corps, it may be effective if it changes the views of only one or two key people.

But over and above the immediate effect of non-recognition or the threat of non-recognition is the symbolic effect that such a policy can have in indicating the political orientation of the United States government. This can be critical in engaging people's sympathies and helping to create goodwill for the United States. This point is worth stressing since the United States so often overlooks the importance of engaging people's sympathies and the significant effect of symbolic action in doing so. The importance of symbolic action in this connection is discussed at greater length elsewhere in this book.

It is sometimes argued that the threat of non-recognition should not be used to forestall a *coup d'état* unless it is absolutely sure that the threat will be effective. If the *coup* occurs despite a U.S. warning, it is argued, then discredit will be cast on the United States. Implicit in this point of view, however, is the sort of absolutism about foreign policy goals that has created so much difficulty for the United States in Vietnam. A sophisticated foreign policy should be conscious not only of those things it wishes to promote or prevent, but also of the magnitude of the costs it is willing to bear in order to bring about its objectives. In South Vietnam, that is, the United States quite reasonably wished to avoid the assumption of power by a Communist government. However, the United States government never made it clear to itself how far it was prepared to go, that is, the costs it was prepared to bear in order to bring about its objective. Thus a commitment was made implying that any costs would be borne, no matter how great they were in human and material terms. This is not only an absurd position, but it is not credible to the adversaries of the United States nor possible to sustain in political or economic terms at home.

The costs the United States should be willing to bear to avoid the assumption of power by a certain type of government in Latin America, let us say, should similarly be limited, perhaps limited to the rather low-cost technique, if a threat of non-recognition prove ineffective, of actual non-recognition for a limited period. This does not mean that United States foreign policy becomes discredited; it only means that a healthy compati-

---

[10]See Martin C. Needler, "Political Development and Military Intervention in Latin America," *American Political Science Review* (September 1966).

bility is maintained between the importance of the objectives sought and the cost the United States is prepared to bear to attempt to meet that objective. U.S. policy-makers of recent years appear to have accepted the view that it is not possible to revive the criterion of automatic recognition of *de facto* governments. However, a new policy has recently been developed which in some ways resembles the policy of *de facto* recognition. Toward the end of the Johnson administration, the practice began that when the question of recognition of a new government in Latin America arose, the United States would take action in consultation with other members of the Organization of American States. In practice, this meant that the United States would recognize new *de facto* governments after several Latin American countries had done so. This is a recipe for the abdication of a role of leadership reminiscent of the favorite motto of that great non-leader Dwight D. Eisenhower: "Be not the first by whom the new is tried, nor yet the last to lay the old aside." As a formula for making oneself inconspicuous, this policy on recognition is much beloved of Foreign Service officers, who are selected, trained, and promoted for cautiousness. It also appeals to other Foreign Service virtues such as that of being non-political, and is especially attractive in that it requires no intellectual effort.

Now exalting intellectual laziness to the status of a foreign policy may be all very well for a very weak country or for one that has no foreign policy objectives to pursue. In the opinion of the present writer, however, the United States does have policy objectives with respect to Latin America; and in pursuit of those objectives it is both legitimate and desirable to use recognition policy along with other tools of intelligent diplomacy.

7

The Implementation of Policy

The way in which a country goes about promoting its foreign policy goals can be as important in determining what actually happens as the content of the goals themselves. Unfortunately, traditional American thinking about cause and effect relations in human behavior is still dominated by the image of the rational and hedonist man of Adam Smith and Jeremy Bentham; in foreign policy, this typically leads to the assumption that foreign leaders will respond automatically to proffered rewards and punishments like B. F. Skinner's white rats. We have had some unfortunate experience with this approach in the attempt to manipulate the behavior of the North Vietnamese by punishment and threats of punishment. In the case of Latin America, Congress has decreed that the United States will automatically cut off aid (often, it should be remembered, not grants but only commercial credit) if a Latin American country buys supersonic planes, or trades with Communist China, or expropriates the property of U.S. citizens without compensation. Aid will be given to countries that draw up comprehensive economic plans, or stabilize their currencies, or overhaul their tax structures. One does not need to appreciate the traditional Hispanic emphasis on personal dignity to see the counter-productive character of the disdain of national autonomy and sovereignty implied in this type of mechanical approach to relations between states.

A mechanical Benthamism or Skinnerism, which conceives of an automatic connection between a stimulus and the appropriate response, overlooks the fact that the will to autonomy of states and statesmen may prevent them from automatically following the path of least pain and most pleasure. It also overlooks the fact that interaction is not confined to a single set of stimuli and responses, but that, over the long term, "affective" relations and perceptions of the true motives and intentions of the other party, both of which influence behavior, are built up out of these experiences. Even if one gets one's way in the short run, the use of strong-arm tactics can have a negative effect on the long-term growth of relations of mutual respect and confidence.

The persistent failure to respect the autonomy of the Latin American states, often by implicit or unconscious behavior, is one of the chief causes of the development of a nationalism that defines itself in anti-United States terms. Thus the United States no longer openly treats the inter-American system, centered on the Organization of American States, as though it were simply the U.S. colonial office; but we still try to bully our way to favorable OAS resolutions, even when these have no practical significance. So long as this and similar tendencies persist, we make it difficult for self-respecting and patriotic Latin Americans to be friends of the United States, and instead attract as our "friends" the servile, the corrupt, and the self-serving.

RELATIONS WITH NON-GOVERNMENTAL ORGANIZATIONS AND INDIVIDUALS

The corrupting influence of this patronizing approach to Latin America is exemplified by such institutions as the American Institute for Free Labor Development, essentially an overseas arm of the AFL-CIO, which collaborates so closely with agencies of the United States government, including the CIA, as to bring itself into complete disrepute. In the AIFLD, trade unionists of the Latin American countries are supposed to receive training in effective techniques and skills of union leadership, yet this is from an institution whose board contains not only representatives of the AFL-CIO but also officials of Standard Oil and Grace Line Shipping, as well as the United States government (even if we overlook the financing of AIFLD activities by the CIA, which is not supposed to be a matter of public knowledge).[1] At the

---

[1] It might also be noted that AIFLD has been further discredited for democratic Latin American unionists because American unionists active in

same time, the *AIFLD Report* proclaims proudly in a headline "Assistant Secretary of State Says AIFLD Reflects U.S. Hemispheric Labor Policy" over a story that begins

> Assistant Secretary of State Charles A. Meyer said that the American Institute for Free Labor Development is a reflection of the United States policy of cooperation "with the free and democratic trade unions of the hemisphere. Indeed the Institute is a mirror of that policy, one that gives substance to our belief in the importance of labor in the development tasks before us."

Of course, many honest and patriotic Latin American unionists will have nothing to do with any organization connected with the AFL-CIO, which faithfully "reflects U.S. policy" to the extent of endorsing the Dominican intervention of 1965.

The "company union" approach to the area of unofficial contacts and non-governmental organizations is particularly regrettable because in this area Americans can help promote the infrastructure of organizations and attitudes supportive of democracy. The State Department's Foreign Leader Exchange Program, under which younger leaders in various fields of endeavor are brought to the United States to travel and make contact with North American colleagues, on the other hand, has proven very successful. But any such attempts must respect the dignity of the people involved, and not appear to demand endorsement of U.S. policies in return for favors and handouts.

RELATIONS WITH REVOLUTIONARY GOVERNMENTS AND PUBLICS

In government-to-government relations, this observation still applies— especially with respect to revolutionary governments. Revolutionary leaders necessarily behave differently from traditional diplomats of the old school, and it would be a mistake to judge their behavior by traditional standards, or to refuse to cooperate with them unless they behave in certain predetermined ways. It is easy to get into a vicious circle of self-reinforcing mutual hostility when a revolutionary leader new to the mores of international society and predisposed to be suspicious of the rich and powerful United States interprets an insistence on diplomatic correctness, for example, as hostility. What the

---

the organization, such as the late Serafino Romualdi and Jay Lovestone, have also collaborated with extreme right-wing organizations, as Victor Reuther has pointed out in a speech cited in *Sane World,* **VI,** 12 (December 1967), p. 2.

United States should attempt to do under these circumstances is to look beneath the surface of the niceties of formal relations to the underlying objectives of the revolutionary government and, without sacrificing essential interests of the United States, try to develop formulas for bringing the two sets of interests and aspirations into harmony.

Even after this is done, there may still remain some areas in which the interests or objectives of the two countries are in irreconcilable opposition; but if a solid ground of common interests has been discovered and built upon and if therefore their good relations appear to both countries to have value, then a compromise arrangement can usually be arrived at for the areas of irreconcilably antagonistic interests—to split the difference, to abide by arbitration, or perhaps to postpone the issue until a more favorable time.

The hard-headed rationalism of the United States' traditional approach to problems of foreign policy has tended consistently to undervalue questions of style, technique, and manner of approach, on the assumption that the most important matter is to decide on objectives, and that the question of how to go about attaining those objectives is a secondary technical question that will take care of itself if a suitable bureaucracy is set up and a large enough amount of money committed. But in the world of international relations there can be no clear-cut separation between a realm of ends and a realm of means. Objectives are not attained once and for all; the reality is rather that of a state of circumstances which one must be continually attempting to modify. Too often, for example, the United States has seen undesirable situations as malignancies calling for surgery whereas in reality what existed was a long-term pathological tendency best worked on by means of diet, exercise, therapy, and measured dosages of vitamins.

The traditional stress on concrete objectives achieved at specific times by the most direct techniques has led to the overlooking of a variety of useful modes of behavior. One of the most useful resources of foreign policy is being able to count on a sympathetic public opinion in other countries. In recognition of this fact the United States spends considerable sums of money on the United States Information Agency and other "information" activities. The most effective influences on foreign opinion, however, are not broadcast propaganda but acts of policy themselves.

Very often the most important acts in determining the attitudes of foreign publics to the United States are not those which have concrete and specific consequences, but those of symbolic value only. Thus the expenditure of millions of dollars in the feeding of school lunches to children is not able to wipe out the recollection that Secretary of State John Foster Dulles pinned a medal on the corrupt and brutal dictator of Venezuela, Marcos Pérez Jiménez. The United States needs to be conscious of the meaning of its actions in terms of the hopes and fears of Latin Americans—and not only of those who happen to be in office at a given moment, but of the masses of the population to whom the governments of the future will be responsive, as mass participation in politics increases and acquires greater force.

In large part, United States policy toward Latin America has been characterized by what we have learned to term "overkill." Sending in the Marines, supporting exile invasions, threatening economic retaliation, though they may be effective in the short run, are, in the long run, counterproductive in destroying the relations of trust necessary to mutual accommodation. But they are also quite inappropriate for the scale and character of relations between the United States and other states of the hemisphere. By virtue of its size and affluence, the United States occupies a natural position of hegemony in the hemisphere. Given the facts of economic and political life, it is clearly in the interest of other countries to maintain good relations with the United States, to maintain a favorable climate for trade and investment if for no other reason. Given this basic circumstance, United States objectives, if they can be achieved at all, can as a rule be attained quite effectively by the use of the less extreme forms of influence.

The more massive techniques of policy that have been used by the United States have been unsound in two respects. In the short run, threats of retaliation, such as those employed against the Peruvian government after it nationalized the International Petroleum Company, force the government to stake its honor on maintaining the confrontation and refusing to compromise. At the same time, over the long range, the image the United States creates of its policies in Latin America becomes that of a reactionary power concerned only to protect vested interests and to obstruct change; so that a reforming government that comes to power finds itself necessarily placed in an anti-United States position. Long-term factors of this type were critical in pointing Fidel Castro's regime, originally indeterminate in policy orientation, in an anti-Yankee direction.

Governments coming to power in Latin America will increasingly be nationalist and socialist. It is essential to the United States interest in maintaining good relations with hemisphere governments, on which our security ultimately rests, that we get out of the box in which we have placed ourselves of being identified as a reactionary force to which any progressive government must necessarily be hostile. Such a shift in "image" is not impossible to achieve, requiring only a consistent line of non-intervention by military means, a willingness to make compromises in cases of the expropriation of private investment, and the demonstration by symbolic acts that the United States is genuinely committed to the cause of political democracy.

Misunderstanding of the character of such symbolic acts often exists. The United States can take a clear political line without intervening in the internal affairs of other countries, and certainly without intervening by forcible means. One can take a clear position against dictatorships in general, or against a given dictatorship in particular, not so that it will immediately be overthrown, or with the implication that, if it is not overthrown, then United States policy is not successful and the United States is discredited. The purpose in the assumption of such a position is rather twofold: to encourage democrats within the country and dishearten the supporters of dictatorship, and perhaps thereby to have an indirect effect on the internal political struggle; and to make clear where the political sympathies of the United States lie so as to encourage favorable attitudes toward the United States on the part of democratic forces.[2]

This is a line of policy that should be generally acceptable in the United States. It did in fact receive general support when it was formulated toward the end of the Eisenhower administration, in the reports to the President of his brother Milton Eisenhower and of the then Vice-President Richard Nixon. To foreswear military intervention, but to continue to discriminate between democracies and dictatorships, was formulated in the succinct slogan "A handshake for the dictator, an *abrazo* for the democrat." One could thus make clear one's political and moral position and wield some indirect influence that was not negligible, without indulging in the discredited practices of intervention.

ECONOMIC ASSISTANCE

In this respect the attempt to affect the immediate situation has to be reconciled with the attainment of long-range objectives, and the techniques used for one set of purposes cannot be allowed to prejudice the other. This point has special application to the question of economic aid. Aid that contributes to economic development seems worthy in itself in alleviating suffering and making a better life possible for the masses. At the same time, more developed economies are likely to be better trading partners for the United States. But it is also true that countries which are developed economically are less violent, and are more likely to be democratic and enjoy constitutional stability.[3] Again, these are desirable ends in themselves, and in addition are congruent with United States interests in a secure world order.

---

[2]"Democratic" is being used here in the broad sense in which it refers to the orientation of social policy as well as to observance of constitutional and legal forms.

[3]See Martin C. Needler, *Political Development in Latin America,* New York: Random House, 1968, Chap. 6; Warren Dean, "Latin American Golpes and Economic Fluctuations, 1823-1966," *Social Science Quarterly*

What this means is that the major thrust of United States economic aid is toward certain long-range objectives—economic development and democratic stability; it would be inappropriate to sacrifice these objectives to the attainment of short-range goals, as when a major development project is halted when United States funds are cut off because of displeasure at an incumbent government's policies. The writer has been impressed by the fact that bitter opponents of the regimes in several countries he has visited have argued that although the United States should cut off military aid or make symbolic gestures of disapproval of those regimes, it should continue to supply economic assistance, which has long-range goals of general benefit to the national population not limited to the success or failure of specific governments. To be sure, this may not always seem a viable policy, if relations between governments should deteriorate. For this reason, as well as for others, it makes sense to channel long-term development aid through multilateral agencies, which can insulate such aid from bilateral disagreements between governments, politically neutralizing it and insuring that it continues to work in the interest of long-run development, both economic and political.

The insulation of development aid from short-run pressures makes particular sense because of the discontinuities in the social and political effects of economic growth. The evidence shows clearly that, in the long run, an economically developed society is more likely to be politically developed in the sense of being democratically responsive, constitutionally authentic, and administratively competent. In the short run, however, the immediate effect of economic change is to introduce strain, and possibly disorder and violence, to the society. Accordingly, it is easy to misinterpret the effects of economic development. One finds the sort of response referred to in Chapter Five: If Colombian society has not been completely reformed and restructured within six years after the Alliance for Progress has begun, then the Alliance must be a failure.

Long-term development aid should be distinguished from short-term or emergency economic assistance to help countries through balance-of-payments and budgetary crises; such aid can be considered more logically as aid to the specific government in power, and whether or not it is extended can legitimately be related to attitudes toward that specific government and toward governments that might possibly replace it. Willingness to extend short-term aid that bolsters a specific government in power, as distinguished from long-term development aid, is logically part of the policy of "the *abrazo*" to democratic rulers, and not that of "the handshake" that dictators receive.

(June 1970); and the address by Robert McNamara to the American Society of Newspaper Editors, Montreal (May 18, 1966), Department of Defense News Release 422-66.

MILITARY ASSISTANCE

A similar distinction needs to be made with regard to military assistance.

The problem here is that the United States has had several objectives in its military assistance program which have frequently operated at cross-purposes to each other. One has been a prudent desire to maintain good relations with all Latin American armies for short-run political reasons. Another has been to coordinate military doctrine, planning, equipment, and training in the event that joint operations become necessary. At the same time, the supply of weapons and other phases of the assistance program have been made to serve short-run political purposes, to bolster governments, or to punish them. In addition, sales of military equipment have been pushed for simple economic reasons.

Now, in the past United States policies on military aid have been counter-productive in several respects. The application by the United States of apparently arbitrary criteria for denying certain classes of weapons to a given country have been regarded as a direct affront to the country's sovereignty and contributed to the worsening of relations, as with the 1968 refusal to allow the Peruvian Air Force to purchase supersonic jets.

United States military missions have established such close working relationships with their Latin American counterparts that they have seemed on occasion to encourage them in political acts that ran counter to the preferences of the State Department and the United States ambassador. The activity of such missions has helped contribute to anti-United States feeling on the part of civilian populations antagonistic to the political roles of their military services and ready to believe that United States national policies are determined exclusively by short-run self-interested military considerations.

The establishment of a defensible policy on military relations and military assistance is not easy. However, such a policy would run along more or less the following lines.[4]

1. There should be no discrimination in the types of arms sold to Latin American countries, except where these have been limited by international treaty. That is, the United States should not get into the position of telling other countries what weapons they do or do not need for their own defense. However, the United States should promote regional and world treaties in which countries mutually agree to limit armaments in their common interest. Thus the United States is now committed not to supply atomic weapons to any of

---

[4]See Luigi Einaudi, *Peruvian Military Relations with the United States,* RAND Corp. (June 1970), p. 43 *et seq.*

the countries of the hemisphere. We should also lend encouragement to arms limitation treaties on a regional basis within Latin America—for example, a naval arms limitation treaty among the South American countries having a Pacific shoreline.

2. However, the United States should not attempt to promote arms purchases, as it does now by vigorous salesmanship motivated by economic as much as by political reasons.

3. United States military missions should be reduced in size and where possible limited to the traditional military attachés at the embassies, with reporting and representational functions primarily. In fact, such a reduction has begun under the Nixon administration, primarily for reasons of economy.

4. Grants of equipment, or sales on concessionary terms, should be made only to governments with which the United States has strong political sympathies and which face immediate and specific military problems. This would be occasional aid on the "lend-lease" model to enable democratic governments to meet emergency situations.

IN CONCLUSION

Criticism of the failings of United States policy typically focuses on problems of aims and objectives. But we need always to be aware that the techniques, manner, and style of policy implementation are not themselves neutral in effect, but are of critical importance in determining the success or failure of policy. This observation applies with especial force in Latin America, where governments change frequently and public opinion is therefore of particular importance.

III

The Recent Past and the Future

8

Counterrevolutionary Policies Under Kennedy and Johnson

The Alliance for Progress embodied a policy that, in its conception if not necessarily in its execution, implied revolutionary change. Yet other actions of the Kennedy administration, which was in reality far less radical than its reputation, had a clearly counterrevolutionary thrust.

THE INVASION OF CUBA

The most spectacular counterrevolutionary action of the Kennedy administration was of course the attempted invasion of Cuba by an exile force organized, financed, and supported by the United States in April 1961. This spectacular failure has been discussed many times, from a variety of perspectives, with the major point at issue usually being why the expedition failed. On this point several theses have been advanced. The technical planning of the effort, it has been argued, was unsound; the timing was wrong; the tactics were inept; and the information on which the enterprise was based was inaccurate. As a consequence of the invasion, for a short time at least, a widespread demand arose to limit the power of the Central Intelligence Agency, which was responsible for the invasion, in order to bring it under civilian control and to limit its "operational" activities, or at least to separate them from those of information-gathering. Given the secrecy surrounding such matters, one does not know how much the situation has been improved, although a healthy skepticism is doubtless justified.

It was easy enough to criticize what has been called "a perfect failure," which took place moreover with such publicity. Although some other cases have become matters of public knowledge, one can only guess at the number of other instances in which the CIA's incompetence and freedom from control have led to serious failures that have been hushed up. The power and freedom from accountability of the CIA is one of the heavy prices the United States pays for having ascribed an absolute priority in its foreign policy to the goal of national security defined as anti-Communism.

A less frequently asked question about the Cuban invasion is not "why did it fail?" but "why was it attempted?" Clearly, today the United States manages somehow to survive even though Fidel Castro remains dictator of Cuba, as he was before the invasion. The invasion caused loss of life, the dishonoring of international commitments of the United States, and a wave of sympathy for Fidel Castro. Why was it attempted?

To some extent mechanical factors were involved, such as that an anti-Castro exile force had already been recruited and trained under the Eisenhower administration. To a great extent, questions of domestic politics were significant, Kennedy wanting to disarm his right-wing critics and to appear a more dynamic leader than his predecessor. Nor should Kennedy's own instinctive anti-Communism be overlooked; the President was a child of the Cold War as much as he was a bridge to the post-Cold War era of mutual *détente* with the Soviet Union.

In addition, some concrete national interests were felt to be threatened by a Communist state in the hemisphere. Although these were not thought through in any detail—the simple presence of Communism was in itself considered a threat to the United States without further analysis—these are worth examining. The threats posed to United States security by a Communist Cuba were two: the possibility of collaboration with the Soviet Union in some form of military threat; and the promotion of subversion and guerrilla warfare in other countries of the area. These "threats," it later transpired (as intelligent prior analysis could have suggested), were in fact very little of a danger. The joint Soviet-Cuban military threat was posed in 1963 by the introduction of Soviet surface-to-surface intermediate range ballistic missiles into Cuba. This actually added to Soviet capabilities only for a brief period since intermediate range missiles in Cuba could do nothing that intercontinental ballistic missiles in Russia, soon to be operational, could not do, except perhaps to save a few minutes' warning time in the event of an attack.[1] President Kennedy chose to interpret the situation as an attempt by

---

[1]Nevertheless, R. R. Rubottom, Jr., an Assistant Secretary of State for Inter-American Affairs under Eisenhower, gave the possible emplacement

the Russians to alter the balance of power and to violate the ground rules of the conduct of the Cold War by encroaching on the United States' immediate security zone. Since no agreed-upon set of rules exists for conducting cold wars, after all, this interpretation of the situation was at least arbitrary, and other equally plausible ones were possible. Under the circumstances of overwhelming United States naval and air power in the Caribbean, Prime Minister Khrushchev had no choice other than to retreat, assuming that he did not want to start World War III—and if he did want to start World War III, he would surely do it by launching a surprise attack over the North Pole, not by gradually escalating a Caribbean conflict in which the United States held all the cards. Although Khrushchev subsequently tried to claim that the whole operation had been a clever maneuver to extract from the United States a commitment not to invade Cuba, it was of course a piece of clumsiness on his part, and was one of the factors that eventually cost him his job. Yet this clumsy and futile maneuver represented the maximum military advantage the Soviet Union could have secured from its alliance with Cuba, in other words the maximum overt military threat that a Communist Cuba could pose for the United States.[2]

The subversion and guerrilla warfare phase of the presumed threat from Cuba was embodied in a string of minor failures, culminating in the major failure of Guevara's campaign in Bolivia. Perhaps the lack of imagination and analytic capacity in both government and public opinion in the United States meant that these possibilities had actually to be acted out before they could be perceived in their true proportions, as of little significance. It remains true that those powers of imagination and analysis have been blunted by the manner in which the "Communist threat" has been perceived.

THE CASE OF BRITISH GUIANA

His impeccably anti-Communist behavior with respect to Cuba still did not free Kennedy from the pressures of anti-Communist opinion in the almost contemporaneous case of British Guiana. This British colony on the

of Soviet missiles as a reason for the Bay of Pigs invasion: "I can also state that one reason for United States support of the anti-Castro elements was precisely the fear that Soviets (sic) would place missiles in Cuba." Review of John N. Plank (Ed.), *Cuba and the United States: Long Range Perspectives,* Washington, D.C.: Brookings Institution, 1967, *The Annals* (March 1968).

[2] Hanson Baldwin tries unconvincingly and with little conviction to make the case that there is still a military threat from Cuba in "A Military Perspective," In John N. Plank, Ed., *op. cit.* His conclusion seems to be that the major contribution of Cuba to the Soviet military position is "psychological."

Atlantic coast of the South American mainland had elected a government whose Prime Minister, Cheddi Jagan, was a Marxist of pro-Soviet sympathies. Kennedy at first tried to distinguish the Jagan case from that of Fidel Castro and of Communist governments elsewhere in the world on the basis that Jagan headed a duly elected government, thus trying to present his position as one of principled support for democracy rather than irrational anti-Communism.[3] When Jagan visited Washington to request economic aid from the United States he undertook explicitly to respect individual freedoms and constitutional procedures, and the United States promised to begin technical studies that would result in the granting of economic aid.[4] But then the pressure of anti-Communist opinion began to take effect and Kennedy began to worry about his prospects for reelection; Dean Rusk took the anti-Communist line, and AID worried about Congressional reaction to the foreign aid program.[5] The preliminary technical studies were dragged out and became pretexts for delay in the actual granting of aid. Finally, the domestic opposition to Jagan, working with officials of the regional labor federation, ORIT, which is dominated by the AFL-CIO (and, according to Jagan, with the CIA and British intelligence) organized a strike that was intended to lead to violence and serve as the pretext for British military intervention in Guiana and the removal of the Jagan government. This occurred according to plan, even though the strike was directed against the implementation of a self-help economic development program, such as was required by the Kennedy government for aid under the Alliance for Progress, drawn up on the advice of Nicholas Kaldor, the British economist who subsequently served as advisor to Harold Wilson's government. One of the more discreditable aspects of this episode is that the Guianan opposition to Jagan, led by the opportunistic Forbes Burnham, had based its campaign on racialist arguments, arousing Afro-Guianans to violence against the East Indians who followed Jagan.

This was a case of rampant anti-Communism, pure and simple. There was no pretense that British Guiana under Jagan's leadership constituted any kind of threat to the security of the United States. Kennedy was here clearly acting against the views of the British government, against his own better

---

[3] "Mr. Jagan who was recently elected Prime Minister in British Guiana is a Marxist, but the United States does not object because that choice was made by honest elections, which he won." Cited in Cheddi Jagan, *The West on Trial: My Fight for Guyana's Freedom,* New York: International Publishers, 1966, pp. 425-426.

[4] An interesting but rather unsatisfactory and somewhat ingenuous account of this visit is given in Arthur M. Schlesinger, Jr., *A Thousand Days: John F. Kennedy in the White House,* New York: Fawcett Crest edition, 1967, pp. 710-713.

[5] *Ibid.,* p. 712.

judgment, and indeed against his own explicit policy statements, out of fear of an irrationally anti-Communist Congressional and public opinion.

GENERAL POLICY APPROACHES UNDER KENNEDY AND JOHNSON

It is worth noting that the actions of this type taken by the Kennedy administration did not form part of a consistent counterrevolutionary orientation. The Kennedy policy of liberal anti-Communism included the encouragement of moderately leftist governments and opposition to their overthrow by military *coups*.[6] The Kennedy administration made particularly strenuous attempts to avoid military *coups* that were in gestation for some time in the Dominican Republic, Honduras, and Peru. In the Dominican Republic, this policy succeeded at least in maintaining Juan Bosch's government in power for some time longer than it would have been able to hold on without the Kennedy policy.[7] In the Peruvian case, the undisguised hostility of the United States to the staging of the *coup* of 1962 seems to have resulted in a reinforcement of those elements within the military *junta* which intended to hold elections the following year, and the weakening of the "military intellectuals" of the *Centro de Altos Estudios Militares* who wanted an indefinite continuation of military rule. The most important effect of the Kennedy policy in Peru, however, was that it made clear where the ideological preferences of the United States lay and thus promoted favorable attitudes toward the United States on the part of the center and center-left.

Under President Johnson, the range of Latin Americans who could sympathize with the policies of the United States was reduced to those on the right and extreme right. What had been under Kennedy a limited and even reluctant anti-Communism became under Johnson a generalized counter-revolutionary tendency that operated against moderates as much as against the extreme left. A man of generally conservative instincts, Johnson not only lacked sophistication in his understanding of the problems of foreign affairs, but, equally unfortunately, lacked the capacity to pick able advisors. It was not until the manifest failure of his Dominican Republic policy that Johnson realized the poor calibre of the advice he had been getting on Latin American affairs and divested himself of those whose counsel he had taken in that

---

[6] A clear and detailed statement of this policy was given by Assistant Secretary Edwin Martin in the *New York Times* (April 18, 1963), apropos of the Guatemalan *coup* that had just taken place.

[7] See the account of this period by Ambassador John Bartlow in his *Overtaken by Events,* Garden City, N.Y.: Doubleday, 1966, especially p. 583.

case–Under-Secretary of State Thomas Mann, Assistant Secretary for Inter-American Affairs Jack Hood Vaughn, and CIA Chief Admiral William Raborn, together with Ambassador to the Dominican Republic W. Tapley Bennett, Jr.–but by then the damage had been done.

Mann, the architect of Johnson's new departures in Latin American policy, had so limited a grasp of the nuances of Latin American politics that, as he told a meeting of United States ambassadors, he saw no difference between Presidents Díaz Ordaz of Mexico, Stroessner of Paraguay, and Paz Estenssoro of Bolivia.[8] Under Mann's leadership, there were to be "no more good guys or bad guys;"[9] in other words, the United States was to abandon its traditional policy of attempting to promote constitutional democracy in the Western hemisphere. Although Mann subsequently denied that this was in fact the intention,[10] the speech in which he did so itself showed his limited grasp of the situation.

What was involved here was not only a failure to support democratic principles, but even a lack of consciousness that such principles were involved in a given situation. The most extraordinary demonstration of this insensitivity had occurred in March 1964, when a combined military-civilian revolt overthrew President João Goulart of Brazil. The United States had every reason to rejoice at Goulart's overthrow. His administration was hopelessly incompetent, vastly corrupt, and likely to result only in a considerable deterioration of an already poor economic situation, together with political chaos and the outbreak of extended violence. Nevertheless, Goulart did happen to be the constitutional president of the republic. Under the circumstances, the obviously correct and proper line to take would have been to maintain a diplomatic silence over the revolt, or perhaps even to break relations temporarily for the sake of demonstrating loyalty to consitutional procedures, while privately making it clear to the new regime that these actions were *pro forma* only.[11] Instead the President of the United States actually sent a telegram of congratulations to the rebel leadership, an action which changed the situation not a whit, except to signal to a startled Latin

---

[8]*New York Times* (March 19, 1964). Mann doubtless intended this assertion as a demonstration of non-ideological "realism" rather than as the confession of ignorance or naïveté which it appears.

[9]*Ibid.*

[10]In his commencement address at the University of Notre Dame (June 7, 1964).

[11]This question is discussed in Thomas Skidmore, *Politics in Brazil, 1930-1964: An Experiment in Democracy,* New York: Oxford Press, 1967, pp. 326-328. See also Robert D. Evans, "The Brazilian Revolution of 1964: Political Surgery Without Anaesthetics," *International Affairs,* **44,** 2 (April 1968).

America that United States pretensions of even nominal support for democracy and constitutional practice were a fraud.

JOHNSON'S POLICY ON MILITARY INTERVENTION

Of course, this type of symbolic act could be called "intervention in internal affairs" only by extension. On the question of direct military intervention in Latin America, the Johnson administration had—at least until the Dominican intervention—an unexceptionable policy. Thomas Mann, the architect of Johnson's Latin American policies, explained it in his speech at the Notre Dame Commencement of June 1964, the year before the Dominican intervention. Referring to the Marine interventions in the Caribbean under Theodore Roosevelt, Taft, and Wilson, Mann said:

> Our interventions were, in the Latin American point of view, patronizing in the extreme. By making the United States the sole judge of Latin America's political morality, they were degrading to proud peoples who believed that, in their own wars of independence, they had earned the right to manage their own affairs—to be masters in their own houses. They produced schismatic tendencies in the inter-American family and brought our relations with Latin America to an all-time low.
>
> These historical experiences suggest two things: unilateral United States interventions in the hemisphere have never succeeded, in themselves, in restoring constitutional government for any appreciable period of time. And they have, in every case, left for our country a legacy of suspicion and resentment which has endured long after our interventions were abandoned as impracticable.[12]

But the irony of hearing these excellent sentiments in the mouth of the man who was subsequently to counsel yet another Marine intervention in the Caribbean is mitigated by reading the "escape clause" that he introduced later in the speech:

> The question of our relations with Communist regimes in this hemisphere is, of course, a separate subject and is beyond the scope of these remarks. It raises separate questions, such as our inherent right of self-defense and measures, under existing

---

[12]"The Democratic Ideal in Our Policy Toward Latin America," Commencement Address by the Honorable Thomas C. Mann, Department of State, mimeo. (June 5, 1964), p. 5.

treaties, to deal with situations which threaten the peace and security of the hemisphere.[13]

In other words, once the anti-Communist nerve is touched any attempt at rational analysis breaks down; other considerations are thrown to the winds as a mumbo-jumbo of "reasons of national security" is cited to justify any reaction panic can dictate.

The failure of the reasoning capacity that issues in "national security" logic of this type produces masterpieces of Orwellian doublethink. Thus further along in his speech Mann gave an illustration of "unilateral intervention for the purpose of forcing constitutional changes in another country," which he opposed. This was a hypothetical attempt to remove from power Carlos Castillo Armas, who had overthrown Jacobo Arbenz Guzmán, the constitutional president of Guatemala; an intervention against Castillo Armas would have been deplorable, said Mann, because it would have restored "a Marxist-Leninist to power against the will of the Guatemalan people." It takes a fine anti-Communist intuition to know that such a restoration of Arbenz would have been "against the will of the Guatemalan people," since, in Mann's own words, "a majority of the Guatemalan people voted in free elections for Arbenz."[14]

The most extraordinary aspect of Mann's citing this case is that it was already a matter of common knowledge that the United States, interpreting the true "will of the Guatemalan people," rather than that simply demonstrated by free elections, had actually organized and financed the Castillo Armas invasion. But the arming and financing of the overthrow of the elected government of Guatemala, having an anti-Communist motive, did of course not constitute "unilateral intervention for the purpose of forcing constitutional changes in another country."

Under-Secretary Mann was placed in the position of having to use words to mean their opposites because he was attempting to draw on a tradition that counseled self-restraint on the part of the United States in order to justify a refusal to act on behalf of the cause of democratic government in the hemisphere, without wishing to forego a policy of active support of anti-Communist insurrections. This is analogous to someone's vigorous defense of the principle of judicial activism when it is a question of striking down social legislation of the New Deal era, that becomes espousal of judicial restraint on questions of the elimination of racial segregation.

Curiously enough, Mann made the point virtually explicit in a subsequent speech at San Diego when—after the Dominican intervention—he

[13]*Ibid.*, p. 7.
[14]*Ibid.*, p. 7.

reaffirmed that although ". . . non-intervention is thought by some to be an obsolete doctrine, I know of no Washington officials who think this way."[15] However, two "areas of confusion" exist.

The first confusion comes from those who say, however obliquely, that it is necessary unilaterally to intervene—'support' is the word most often used—in favor of political parties of the non-Communist left. With all respect, this thesis is justified by the same rhetoric that was used to justify our unilateral interventions in the past.[16]

On the other hand, asked the Under-Secretary rhetorically,

Are Communists free to intervene while democratic states are powerless to frustrate that intervention? This is not so much a question of intervention as it is of whether weak and fragile states should be helped to maintain their independence when they are under attack by subversive elements responding to direction from abroad.[17]

Translated into operational terms, thus, Mann's policy of "non-intervention" apparently means that the United States should not "support" governments of the democratic left—that is just the same as intervention; however, sending in the Marines against movements of the left—democratic or not—is "not so much a question of intervention" and is thus quite all right. Thus it is "intervention" to give Juan Bosch any support, even only moral or financial support, after he has been elected by 60 percent of the Dominican voters; it is not "intervention" to send in the Marines to prevent him from being returned to power by a popular uprising after a corrupt and brutal military has removed him.

The Dominican intervention, and the events which led up to it, are worthy of examination and contemplation in some detail, not only because of their far-reaching effect on Dominican politics or their impact on U.S. relations with Latin America, but also because of what they reveal about how foreign policies are conceived and put into execution in the United States; about the distortions of perception and evaluation to which an exclusive emphasis on anti-Communism can lead; and about the moral and political costs of ill-informed and ill-considered policy.

---

[15] Address by the Honorable Thomas C. Mann before the Annual Meeting of the Inter-American Press Association at San Diego, Calif., Department of State, mimeo. (October 12, 1965), p. 1.

[16]*Ibid.,* p. 1.

[17]*Ibid.,* p. 2.

9

The Dominican Intervention

In 1965 the United States again undertook the kind of political operation that had long been thought possible only in the bad old days. As though the year were 1910 and the President William Howard Taft, the Marines were ordered into a Caribbean country.[1]

Viewed in a long-term perspective, the tragic element in the Dominican situation, as it had evolved since Trujillo met his end on a deserted section of the Santo Domingo-San Cristóbal highway, was that an unexpectedly promising beginning for a democratic chapter of Dominican history had been brought to an untimely close when Juan Bosch was overthrown seven months after he had taken office as President. The victory of Bosch, a representative of the democratic left, a figure of hemispheric significance almost unique among Dominicans for his understanding of democracy and his devotion to democratic processes, in an election exemplary for its honesty and high level of participation, had always seemed "too good to be true," given the barbarous history of the Dominican Republic. The United States had lent Bosch conspicuous support at the time of his assumption of office, in both

---

[1]Except where a source is specifically cited, the material in this chapter was synthesized from a wide range of sources, including the Dominican press and oral interviews conducted by the author on visits to the Dominican Republic. For published sources, see the bibliography at the end of the book, pp. 121-123.

moral and material senses, partly to counteract the feeling that the U.S. had favored his conservative opponent, Viriato Fiallo, but also because Bosch represented the progressive forces of the democratic left with which the Kennedy administration wished to be identified. But given the Dominicans' absolute lack of experience with constitutional government and the habituation of military officers to graft-taking as by right, it was all but inevitable that right-wing elements in the military and business would not long be able to tolerate an honest reform government, and Bosch's lack of skill as politician and administrator made their task easier.

However, in itself ineptitude does not make a very powerful case for a *coup d'état,* and several myths were propagated to create a climate of opinion in which Bosch could be overthrown, and to justify the *coup* retroactively. These were on the whole the standard arguments which are made under such circumstances in Latin America. In other words, the primary charge leveled against Bosch was that he was a "Communist," or perhaps a pro-Communist, or at any rate was "soft on Communism." This allegation was propagated in the United States by journalists who should have known better; paradoxically, not only was Bosch a favorite target as an "imperialist puppet" for Fidel Castro, but nothing in Bosch's personal or political background could legitimately give rise to the slightest doubt that he was anything other than a sincere democrat of the moderate left.[2] Ironically enough, the major target for the charge that Bosch was surrounded by Communists was Sacha Volman, in effect the head of the agency involved in the conception and to some extent the implementation of Bosch's social and economic reform program; yet Volman had formerly been the head of the Institute for Political Education in Costa Rica which, it subsequently transpired, had actually been an unwitting recipient of funds from the C.I.A. Of course, in the lexicon of the Dominican right wing, a Communist was anyone who wanted to introduce social change, and the term was applied to President Kennedy and Pope John XXIII as well as to Juan Bosch.

While the military controlled the political situation following the *coup* that overthrew President Bosch, they had no interest in the day-to-day running of the government and so a provisional civilian *junta* was formed, called "the triumvirate," which was to govern the country until new presidential elections could be held. Because of the difficulties inherent in the country's economic and political situation, together with the problems presented by the *de facto* domination of the military, the original personnel of the triumvirate was totally replaced during the first year of its existence.

---

[2]This aspect of the situation is explored thoroughly by Theodore Draper in a two-part article, "Defamation: U.S. Intelligence Vs. Juan Bosch," *The New Republic* (February 19 and 26, 1966).

As the personnel of the triumvirate changed, one of its members gradually attained a dominant position not only within the group itself, but to some extent even vis-à-vis the military. This was Donald Reid Cabral, a businessman whose Scottish father had married into a wealthy and prominent Dominican family. Donald Reid came to dominate the government so much that eventually when one of the members of the triumvirate resigned he was not replaced, while the second surviving member of the abbreviated triumvirate, Ramón Cáceres Troncoso, functioned more or less as an assistant to Reid. By the beginning of 1965, it had become clear that Donald Reid would himself be the leading candidate for president in the election scheduled for September of that year.

One aspect of Reid's strategy to secure the presidency was the attempt to create a popular following for his less than charismatic personality. This involved such things as descending by helicopter on the peasants of the interior bearing titles to land they had been given under the land reform program inherited by the triumvirate from the Bosch government. A second phase of Reid's electoral preparations consisted of keeping out of the country its two most popular figures, Bosch and Joaquín Balaguer. Balaguer had been serving as puppet president when Trujillo was assassinated, and had gained great popularity with the masses by distributing some of Trujillo's possessions to them (cab drivers were given ownership of the vehicles they drove, for example). Although Reid never publicly stated that neither Bosch nor Balaguer would be allowed to run for president, it was taken for granted that the prohibition on the return of either to the country imposed earlier would remain in effect.

Reid Cabral even moved, shrewdly and with indirection, to reduce the power of the central figures in the military hierarchies. Secretary of the Armed Forces Elby Viñas Román was "kicked upstairs" to an honorific post in Washington. Even the powerful chief of police, Belisario Peguero, was eased out of office by a series of complicated administrative reorganizations. The only one of the old military president-makers who continued to tower over the scene was thus Brigadier General Elías Wessín y Wessín.

Wessín y Wessín, an extreme, even fanatical, "anti-Communist," who had been the key figure in the overthrow of Juan Bosch, was commander of the Center for Armed Forces Training (CEFA). CEFA disposed of a powerful array of land and air forces and was based at San Isidro, near Santo Domingo; it had been created by Trujillo to serve as the ultimate control over the danger of military insurrection, and in Trujillo's day it had been under the command of his son Ramfis. Appreciating San Isidro's crucial position, Wessín had elected to retain command of CEFA rather than assume the presidency at the overthrow of Bosch.

Needless to say, a great many military officers felt extremely uneasy as they saw the strength of Reid Cabral's position grow, which even raised the possibility of their being placed under effective civilian control, a situation that would have been without precedent in Dominican history. Armed forces aggrievement was further intensified by cautious moves Reid Cabral made in the direction of curbing the armed forces' privilege of importing articles duty-free for sale in military commissaries. This had been made the basis of a contraband racket that had grown to such proportions that it had a significant adverse effect on the country's balance of payments, a particularly sensitive area because of the substantial worsening of the Dominican Republic's trade position, due to a combination of several factors. For a considerable period following the overthrow of Juan Bosch, income from tourism had dropped in response to the unsettled political situation; the rice crop had been small, which made it necessary to import this basic ingredient of the Dominican diet; sugar production also dropped considerably, due to adverse weather conditions, and world sugar prices hit new lows in the face of a heavy oversupply on the world market. The Republic's foreign exchange position was so severely affected that the International Monetary Fund, early in 1964, recommended that the Dominican peso be devalued by 50 percent. Reid Cabral did not accept the IMF recommendation, but he did embark on drastic monetary stabilization measures. These included the cancelling of Christmas bonuses for government workers and the cutting of payrolls in the sugar industry, 60 percent of which was government-owned—a legacy of the Trujillo era—and Reid even dared to cut the military budget. It was ironic that Reid Cabral, who was a relatively competent administrator and economic manager, should have been brought low because of economic difficulties. He could thus join Arturo Frondizi, Jânio Quadros, and José María Velasco Ibarra as Latin American leaders of the early 1960's whose end had been hastened by the political complications of their attempts at monetary stabilization; the treatment may be successful, but the doctor dies.

It should be noted that almost all political groups were alienated from the Reid Cabral regime, even before their disaffection was heightened first by the deteriorating economic situation and then by the means taken to alleviate it. Supporters of Juan Bosch grew desperate as it became apparent that Bosch would not be allowed to return to the country and compete in the September presidential elections, while younger followers of Bosch's *Partido Revolucionario Dominicano* started to desert to parties on the extreme left as the PRD seemed not to be an effective vehicle for opposing the Reid Cabral government. Balaguer's supporters, who included a substantial group of military officers, were likewise disappointed that their man would not be allowed to become president. Other military groups were disaffected over the cut in the military budget, the beginning of attempts to end the contraband racket, the possibility of the further reduction of the power of the military by a Reid Cabral strengthened in authority by virtue of popular election, or by a combination of these motives. Only some upper-status business groups close to Reid Cabral remained loyal as the opposition to him crystallized and came to a head.

Interestingly enough, it was possible for several of the anti-Reid Cabral groups, although of very different orientations,[3] to pursue parallel courses in plotting against him on the basis of the assumption that Reid's government would be succeeded by a military *junta* that would prepare for elections in which both Bosch and Balaguer would be allowed to run. The conspiratorial groups could moreover count on at least the neutrality of Wessín y Wessín, if not his active collaboration.

The revolt was precipitated when, on the morning of April 24, the army Chief of Staff, General Marcos Rivera Cuesta, attempted to arrest three of the leading figures conspiring against Reid, and was himself instead arrested by them. That afternoon a group of rebels seized the government radio station long enough to broadcast a bulletin that the triumvirate had been overthrown. As the masses took to the streets to demonstrate and celebrate, Donald Reid realized, after the United States declined to intervene on his behalf,[4] that there was no hope for him and made no attempt to offer resistance. At this point the decision was taken which led, not to a provisional *junta* that would tolerate the activities of all groups, but instead to civil war and foreign intervention. Pro-Bosch conspirators, suspecting that the generals who had overthrown Juan Bosch would not in fact allow free elections that might result in Bosch's return to power (on another occasion a colonel who had participated in the conspiracy against Bosch remarked, "If Bosch ever comes back he will throw me into jail so deep I will never find my way out") decided to operate on the premise that Bosch was still legally president of the Republic. Accordingly, a "constitutional" government was established in the National Palace once that had been seized, headed by the official of the Bosch era next in the line of constitutional succession, Rafael Molina Ureña, who had been president of the Chamber of Deputies. The demands formulated by this government were the return of Bosch from his exile in Puerto Rico and his resumption of office, and the restoration of the PRD-drafted constitution of 1963. At the same time pro-Bosch elements

---

[3]Abraham Lowenthal argues that ideological position was secondary in importance to simple desire for power, if not altogether irrelevant. "The Dominican Republic: The Politics of Chaos," Arpad von Lazar and Robert R. Kaufman (Eds.), *Reform and Revolution: Readings in Latin American Politics,* New York: Allyn and Bacon, 1969, pp. 41-42.

[4]J. William Fulbright, *The Arrogance of Power,* New York: Vintage (Random House), 1967, p. 86.

among the younger military officers began to arm civilians in the capital, most of whom seemed to identify themselves with the "constitutionalist" cause. As might have been imagined, this undisciplined army of civilians created the chaos which was to make such an impression on the United States Ambassador, W. Tapley Bennett, Jr., when he returned to his post on April 27 from Washington. The hated police, especially, were victimized by the population, and the police force seemed to disappear as its members changed their uniforms for civilian clothes to avoid the fate of several of their number who were lynched by angry mobs.

As the revolt became transformed from a broad anti-Reid movement to one that was simply pro-Bosch, Balaguer supporters deserted it, some of them joining General Wessín y Wessín at the San Isidro Air Base. Wessín, who had not raised a finger to save Reid Cabral, now went into action, ordering a tank advance against the city, which began on April 25, and strafing the city from the air on that day and the one following. By April 27, many of the leading middle class figures who had held office under Bosch and were now prominent in the rebellion, including Acting President Molina Ureña, believed it to be defeated and a delegation of them requested that Ambassador Bennett arrange a cease-fire. Simultaneously, Juan Bosch made the same request to the papal nuncio. The attempt to reach a cease-fire, which would have meant a political stalemate and compromise, was rudely rejected by Bennett, one of the crucial mistakes made by United States officials. In fact, United States authorities had already decided to back Wessín y Wessín, as a result of sensationalist mis-reporting to Washington by the embassy and by U.S. intelligence in Santo Domingo of supposed Communist leadership of the rebels, and of rebel atrocities. Following Bennett's rejection of their request for mediation, most of the constitutionalist leaders, including Molina Ureña, sought refuge in foreign embassies. Some minor figures, led by Colonel Francisco Caamaño Deñó, felt this dishonorable and resolved to fight on to the end. Meanwhile Wessín, confident in his assurance of American support, refused the papal nuncio's request for a cease-fire and determined instead to crush the revolution, on the same day (April 28) naming a provisional government of three military officers.

But the assumption that the constitutionalist cause was defeated proved premature. The forces of the military *junta* fought half-heartedly in the face of overwhelming popular opposition, as evidences of support for the constitutionalist cause came from the provinces, and as the constitutionalist forces were now led by those who had determined to stay and fight to the end. The latter included members of the three extreme leftist parties.

The largest and most important of these was the 14th of June Movement, made up principally of young people of Castroite orientation. Also on the far left was the Movimiento Popular Dominicano, which had gotten its start when Trujillo decided that a visible domestic Communist party would strengthen his hand in dealings with the United States, and which was now oriented to Peking. The least radical of the three was the Popular Socialist Party, a traditional Communist party loyal to Moscow, which subsequently changed its name to the Dominican Communist Party. However, the leading roles in the constitutionalist movement were still taken by members of the PRD, Bosch's party; by Christian Democrats of the Partido Revolucionario Social Cristiano, a group whose political views paralleled those of the PRD closely; and by several individuals of ambiguous political backgrounds who had been brought together fortuitously in the course of the fighting. Among the latter were the two key figures in this phase of the conflict, Colonel Francisco Caamaño Deñó and Hector Aristy. Caamaño Deñó, a burly 32-year-old, had assumed command of the rebel forces as the ranking military officer after its better-known leaders had quit the field on April 27, an act which was subsequently legitimized when the surviving members of Bosch's Congress available in the rebel-held zone met to elect Caamaño "Provisional President," on Bosch's nomination. That Caamaño should have emerged as rebel leader was typical of the shifts in political allegiance that have been notable in the Dominican Republic from the Trujillo era on. Before his rebirth as revolutionary hero, Caamaño Deñó, the U.S.-educated son of a Trujillo police chief, had been noted as head of the hated *Cascos Blancos,* the white-helmeted riot squad used to break up political rallies. Aristy had previously been affiliated with the center-right Partido Liberal Evolucionista, headed by one of the two survivors of the group that had assassinated Trujillo, Luis Amiama Tió. Aristy served as Caamaño's leading political advisor; but on major questions the constitutionalists followed the advice of Juan Bosch, with whom they were in constant contact by telephone.

As the tide again turned on April 28, it was now the forces of Wessín y Wessín that seemed in imminent danger of collapse. At this point Ambassador Bennett discovered the danger to American lives—although no American lives had been lost during the most violent periods of the days preceding—and requested the dispatch of Marines. The Marines landed the night of April 28, and while they did supervise the evacuation of American and other foreign nationals, and establish an "international zone" embracing most of the foreign embassies and the Hotel Embajador, it was clear that their primary mission was to prevent the victory of the rebel forces. Transfixed by the possibility that a rebel victory would mean the conversion of the Dominican Republic into "another Cuba," the American embassy and the Washington authorities appeared greatly impressed by any evidence, no matter how scanty or unreliable, that Communists were involved in the uprising. One of the major items of evidence of this type was a list compiled by the CIA of fifty-eight "Communists" active in the rebel camp. It is less important that this list contained duplications and cases of mistaken identity, or that some of those listed were actually in prison or out of the country during the uprising,[5] than that Americans had become so used to thinking in terms of conspiratorial demonology that the mere presence of fifty-eight Communists in a force of tens of thousands was thought necessarily to imply Communist domination or control.

The effect of the intervention and its creation of a neutral zone between the constitutionalist forces and those of the military *junta* was in the first instance to halt the fighting, which meant the prevention of the constitutionalist victory that had then appeared imminent. In the second place, the intervention vastly strengthened the morale of the Wessín forces and led to the relapse into apathy or into formal allegiance to the *junta* of many who had earlier been inclined towards the rebel cause. In bottling up the constitutionalist forces in downtown Santo Domingo, thirdly, the intervention made it possible for the *junta* to extend its control over the remainder of the country. The situation thus settled into a stalemate punctuated by occasional resumptions of fighting, by sniping, and by the torture and killing of political opponents and suspected opponents of the *junta* forces within the territory they now controlled.

The transformation of the military *junta* took place shortly after the arrival of the Marines, and clearly under American auspices, in a pathetic attempt to make it more palatable to the population and more effective politically. Placed at the head of the new *junta* was the well-known, and to many Americans in official positions highly acceptable, figure of General Antonio Imbert Barrera. Imbert had long cultivated good relations with the Embassy, especially its military attachés, and Americans half conversant with Dominican politics might assume that he would be agreeable to the military because of his rank, on the one hand, and yet acceptable to the democratic forces as the other survivor, besides Amiama, of the group that assassinated Trujillo. But the image which Imbert projected was rather more complex than this. In the first place Imbert's military status was ambiguous. He had not been a professional soldier, but was given his military rank by the provisional Council of State that had succeeded Balaguer, partly as an honor and partly to provide him with a bodyguard against Trujillist attempts at revenge. In the second place, although Imbert had, to be sure, earned the gratitude of the country as one of the tyrannicides, he was also remembered by many Dominicans as a brutal and corrupt provincial governor under Trujillo, whose

---

[5]For the farcical aspects of this famous list, see Theodore Draper, "The Dominican Crisis: A Case Study in American Policy," *Commentary*, December 1965, pp. 52-55.

disaffection with the dictator was based more on personal than on public motives. In the third place, it later transpired that Tony Imbert had been hedging his bets and had not only been shooting quail with the American military attaché, but had also been secretly in contact with the 14th of June Movement and had even enabled them to secure weapons and ammunition.[6]

The realization that Imbert was something other than Sir Galahad went hand in hand with second thoughts in Washington, as the more liberal voices within the administration began to make themselves heard and as the generally unfavorable impact of Latin American reaction to the intervention was felt. Rather pathetically baffled by the discounting of the famous list of fifty-eight Communists which he had even cited on nationwide television, President Johnson ordered the F.B.I. into the Dominican Republic to check on the accuracy of the reports he had received from the C.I.A. At the same time, implicit support of the Imbert *junta* gave way to an undermining of the *junta* as a prerequisite to the negotiation of a compromise solution that would in effect embody the goals of the "responsible" democratic left of the type of those leaders who had taken refuge in foreign embassies on April 27. These negotiations were at first conducted by various presidential emissaries, including at one point Assistant for National Security Affairs McGeorge Bundy. After the military intervention was half-heartedly inter-Americanized by the O.A.S., a Brazilian commander and token contingents of Brazilian, Paraguayan, Nicaraguan, and Honduran troops being added to the more than 20,000 American soldiers in the Republic, negotiations were conducted by an O.A.S. team whose key figure was U.S. Ambassador Ellsworth Bunker.

Two major difficulties facing a successful peace negotiation had to be overcome. In the first place, an individual had to be found to serve as provisional president who would be more or less acceptable to both sides and whose character and antecedents would themselves be a guarantee of fair treatment to all, and of evolution toward a resumption of constitutionality. In the second place, a source of pressure other than a resumption of the fighting had to be found to provide the extra margin of persuasive power that would be needed to get each contender actually to surrender his capacity to fight to the new provisional government that was to be formed.

After the names of several personalities of center-left orientation had been canvassed and rejected in turn, the person found least objectionable to the two contending sides was Héctor García Godoy, a career diplomat who

---

[6]See Luis Homero Lájara Burgos, "Antonio Imbert and U.S. Anti-Communist Intervention in the Dominican Republic," in Norman Thomas (Ed.), *Dominican Republic: A Study in the New Imperialism,* New York: Institute for International Labor Research, n.d. (1965). See p. ii of Thomas's introduction to this pamphlet for a list of additional sources on this point.

had served under every recent Dominican government from Trujillo to Bosch and thus had connections over a wide spectrum of political opinion. García Godoy's highest government post had been as Foreign Minister under Bosch and he had demonstrated loyalty to Bosch by refusing a post under the government which had overthrown him, thus ending his long government career. García Godoy further qualified by his activities since the overthrow of Bosch; he had become associated with the management of the sugar industry, thus becoming widely known and well regarded among the business interests of the center and center-right.

The second problem was amenable of solution up to a point. After the United States' intervention, Washington had offered to assume the responsibility of meeting the payrolls of both of the contending "governments" until the situation was normalized. The constitutionalists wisely declined; but Imbert, perhaps overestimating the strength of his position and in any case taking over the bulk of the pre-existing government apparatus, accepted the American offer. Having become dependent upon American funds, the Imbert government was thus fairly easily brought to heel when these were cut off after he showed reluctance to accept the García Godoy solution. Imbert's position had also steadily been undercut by the negotiators, who bypassed him and dealt directly with the military commanders on whom his position depended. The constitutionalist forces, less reluctant to accept a solution that would probably tend ultimately toward the satisfaction of their initial demands, by resulting in an election that would return Bosch to power, were persuaded of the weakness of their position at a crucial point in the negotiations by a foray into their territory by the inter-American force, ostensibly designed to put an end to sniping, which easily steamrollered the resistance made by the constitutionalists.

Even after the agreement was concluded and the García Godoy government installed, on September 3, opposition from extremists in both camps continued. Although Caamaño Deñó faithfully collaborated with the new government, 14th of June elements resisted by arms the reincorporation of the former constitutionalist zone into the territory under the authority of the new national government, and several people were killed in the resultant fighting. At the same time, the extreme right became disaffected as it realized the political tendency which the new government would inevitably follow, as indicated by García Godoy's appointment to his cabinet of two leading members of Caamaño Deñó's "constitutionalist" government, Franklyn Domínguez as Minister of Information, and Manuel Ramón Morel Cerda as Attorney General. The key troublemaker on the right was eliminated, however, when the government succeeded in deporting General Wessín y Wessín to exile in the United States, not without the aid of a phalanx of troops from the inter-American force.

Against all odds, the García Godoy government complied with its mandate, staying in office until it had held elections and turned over power to a new President—Joaquín Balaguer, who defeated the other ex-Presidents running, Bosch and Rafael Bonnelly. Bosch had hurt his chances by campaigning only by radio speeches from his home, presumably because of his fear of assassination, thus reinforcing doubts about his courage raised by his failure to return to the island at the time of the revolt of April. A precarious peace was thus restored to the Dominican Republic, and the United States government was spared the agonizing decisions that would have faced it had Bosch been again elected and again overthrown.

Although President Johnson never acknowledged publicly that he had been wrong in ordering the Marines into the Dominican Republic, and in fact repeatedly asserted the contrary, his subsequent actions spoke almost as loud as an explicit confession of error would have done. Within fourteen months of the invasion, none of the principals involved in advising Johnson to send in the Marines remained in their jobs, although some transfers represented nominal promotions. Tapley Bennett's tour as ambassador was cut short and he was reassigned as Ambassador to Portugal. The head of the Caribbean Affairs office, Kennedy M. Crockett, became deputy chief of mission in Costa Rica, something less than a key position. Jack Hood Vaughn, Assistant Secretary for Inter-American Affairs, returned to the politically less sensitive Peace Corps. Under-Secretary Thomas Mann, who had even been tipped by insiders as a future Secretary of State, instead left government service for private business. And Admiral Raborn was retired after just a year as the shortest-lived head of the C.I.A. since its founding.

For the United States, the episode threw into sharp relief a whole series of unpleasant truths. The inferior quality of much of the country's representation abroad had again been emphasized, together with the limited ability of the C.I.A. in the gathering and evaluation of intelligence. The conservative nature of President Johnson's reflexes had been made clear.

But the major failing was that of understanding—both of desirable United States policy objectives, and of the forces at work in Latin American politics.

Apart from the immediate and obvious costs of the Dominican intervention—the loss of life, the throwing away of the credit with moderate opinion in Latin America earned at some cost by the Kennedy administration, the public demonstration of the incapacity of the foreign-policy making apparatus of the United States—the future of Dominican politics was prejudiced in two crucial ways. First, young democratically-minded Dominicans who had supported the PRD in the attempt to secure basic structural change within a democratic framework were driven to an extreme leftist and anti-Yankee position. This appeared to be true also of Caamaño

Deñó and to some extent of Juan Bosch himself, both of whom had had direct and bitter personal experience of official Yankee duplicity, stupidity, and lack of concern. Caamaño Deñó served for a time as military attaché in London and finally disappeared mysteriously, apparently going to Cuba, and from his exile in Spain, Bosch announced that he now believed that only dictatorship could bring progress to the Dominican Republic. Thus an "anti-Communist" intervention had the effect of strengthening "Communism."

Second, the United States intervention had saved the traditional armed forces from being defeated and disbanded. To appreciate the folly involved here, one has to understand that the Dominican armed forces were Trujillo's men, corrupt, brutal—in many cases, no more than licensed gangsters. The money that these people drain away in salaries, graft, extortion, and smuggling is less important than the preservation of their veto power over any government that is reforming, libertarian, or even honest. The only way for decency to have had a chance in the Dominican Republic was for this monster to have been destroyed. That opportunity was itself destroyed by the United States, and in the days after the Marines landed the monster claimed its victims as many who had fought on the constitutionalist side or even were merely known to be convinced democrats were killed, often after torture. Six years after the intervention, these assassinations were still taking place. Many of those who were not killed and who did not go over to the extreme left were scared into exile or silence, thus depriving the center and moderate left of their leadership.

The long-term effect of the intervention, in itself, was thus to strengthen the extremes, especially the forces of brutality and gangsterism. After the intervention the United States tried to recoup its losses by mounting in the republic the most expensive aid program per capita outside Vietnam, administered by what Dominicans have called a "parallel government" of USAID officials. Yet three years after the intervention per capita national income had still not climbed back up to the pre-intervention level. Political losses cannot be measured as accurately as economic; but there is no doubt that they were very great indeed.

10

Nixon and Latin America:
A Preliminary Assessment

As in some areas of domestic affairs, the Nixon approach to Latin America was marked more by inactivity than by positive acts—a sort of "benign neglect," to use Daniel Patrick Moynihan's unfortunate but revealing phrase. To a large extent, therefore, understanding Nixon's Latin American policies becomes a question of examining public statements rather than overt actions; with the proviso that an absence of positive actions is itself a policy.

President Nixon took office without a clearly formulated Latin American policy; Latin America had a low salience on his foreign policy horizon, dominated as it was by his primary concern, U.S.-Soviet relations. The same statement could be made of his key foreign policy advisor, Henry Kissinger. Yet there were certain predilections in Nixon's basic set of orientations on foreign policy questions that provided the framework within which his policy on Latin America evolved.

As it happened, however, that set of orientations, as applied to Latin America, contained essentially contradictory elements. On the one hand, Nixon's reaction against the messianism of the Kennedy Latin American policies presaged a "low profile," consistent with Nixon's policies elsewhere. This tendency was reinforced by the traditional Republican aversion to high levels of government spending, made more acute by the financial stringencies growing out of the Vietnam war and rising costs in other federal programs. Clearly, spending for "foreign aid" on the scale that obtained during the early

Kennedy years was out of the question, and in any case the feeling in Congress was that large-scale spending had been ineffective in contributing to the objectives of U.S. policy.

At the same time, however, there were several elements in Nixon's mental set that pointed instead to an active and interventionist policy. The crusading anti-Communism of his early years and of the foreign policies of the Eisenhower administration in which he had served had not altogether been abandoned. Moreover, a key point of friction with Latin American governments, one on which arguments for interventionist policies have been based, was the protection of the interests of U.S. investors, a concern necessarily close to business-oriented Republicans.

Partially for guidance, but at least as importantly in order to demonstrate his concern, one of the first things Nixon did as president was to ask his old rival, the governor of New York and former Assistant Secretary of State for Inter-American Affairs under Franklin Roosevelt, Nelson Rockefeller, to make a tour of Latin America and return with policy recommendations. Some cynics implied that the President's request was not entirely free from malice, remembering the tomatoes and rotten eggs that had greeted Nixon himself on his tour of Latin America ten years before. There were indeed hostile demonstrations against the Rockefeller visits and in some countries they were cancelled or drastically shortened. The curious and thought-provoking parallel that John F. Kennedy had asked Adlai Stevenson to make a Latin American tour on his behalf at the beginning of his own presidential term went unnoticed.

The bulky report resulting from Rockefeller's visits to Latin America contained extensive analyses of some aspects of the area's social, economic, and political reality as well as a series of proposals for action.[1] The activist mood of the report reflected a strenuous Republicanism of the Theodore Roosevelt variety rather than the low-profile restraint of the Coolidge or Hoover type more congenial to President Nixon. Most of the report made good sense, and many of its recommendations were of a non-controversial or technical character.

In a generally sound analysis of the political situation, the report laid especial emphasis on the growth of nationalism. It reaffirmed U.S. support for democracy in the hemisphere, correctly pointing out that the United States was likely to have more in common, and to collaborate more effectively, with democratic governments. In terms reminiscent of Nixon's

---

[1]The versions of the report most readily available are "Quality of Life in the Americas," published by the Agency for International Development, and *The Rockefeller Report on the Americas,* Chicago: Quadrangle Books, 1969.

own recommendations to President Eisenhower of ten years before, Governor Rockefeller argued that the United States should find ways of helping the peoples of Latin America without necessarily embracing their governments (a recommendation that hardly seemed consistent with the widely circulated photograph of Rockefeller with the Haitian dictator, François Duvalier, which gave a great boost to the latter's prestige. The existence of progressive elements among Latin American military forces was stressed, and it was suggested that the United States find ways of working with these progressive elements and not insulting them. The recognition or non-recognition of new governments should be purged of its implications of approval or disapproval. The United States should remove the encumbrances on its economic aid to the countries of the area, and should encourage private investment. It should support commodity agreements and expand trade, trying to secure a system of preferences for the products of underdeveloped countries in the markets of developed countries.

In the report these forward-looking suggestions coexisted with several more traditional concerns. Heavy emphasis was laid on "the subversive capabilities of Communist forces" and the report stated explicitly: "Clearly, the opinion in the United States that Communism is no longer a serious factor in the Western hemisphere is thoroughly wrong."[2] A "Western Hemisphere Security Council" should coordinate action against such subversion and the United States should cooperate closely with the Latin American military, a collaboration which, the Governor professed to believe, influenced Latin American armies in a democratic direction.

Latin America should of course receive more attention in United States government circles, said the report, and Rockefeller proposed to institutionalize such concern by creating a Cabinet-level Secretary for Western Hemisphere Affairs, and placing economic aid under the supervision of a new agency located in the Executive Office of the President.

Many of these ideas represented common sense learning from the palpable mistakes of the past, as in the proposals for the removal of encumbrances on economic aid, and the expansion of trade. The proposal for administrative upgrading of government offices having to do with Latin America was predictable, having been a staple of such recommendations for a long time—as was also the failure to implement the proposal in practice.

With all its merits, however, the report contained three major defects. The first was its concentration on a "Communist threat" whose exact character was never clearly specified. No attempt was made to distinguish between Communist and non-Communist revolutionaries, for example; yet in the world to be created by the Rockefeller report, if the United States were

---

[2]See p. 35 in the Quadrangle edition.

to collaborate with the Latin American military in developing counter-subversive strategies it would no doubt find itself accepting the extremely broad characterizations of people as Communists (and thus *ipso facto* foreign agents) typically made by the Latin American military, which have been precisely one of the causes of the policy disasters of the past. In the second place, acceptance of the perfectly correct point that some members of the military today have progressive orientations is, in the Rockefeller report, allowed to eclipse the fact that the majority of Latin American armies today, as traditionally, continue to serve as bulwarks of an unjust status quo. Finally, a critical defect of the report is that it does not face the problem of what to do about the expropriation of the property of U.S. nationals by Latin American governments. This omission is especially curious in view of the stress on the growth of nationalism contained in the introduction to the report, the attention to economic matters throughout, and the premise that private investment has an important role to play, in partnership with the U.S. government, in developing Latin America. A hint of how Rockefeller might handle expropriation cases may be contained in the statement, "U.S. national interests must supersede those of any domestic special interest group in the conduct of Western hemisphere relations,"[3] but the point is not elaborated, and no specific recommendations are made.

When President Nixon came to make his first general statement on his administration's policies toward Latin America, in his address to the Inter-American Press Association of October 31, 1969, his recommendations drew on the Rockefeller proposals, as he explicitly acknowledged. The general approach of the policies embodied in Nixon's speech, "Action for Progress for the Americas,"[4] was clearly "low profile." Heavy stress was laid on respect for the "national identity and national dignity" of other countries of the hemisphere and the President stated his preference for multilateral action within the inter-American system over unilateral action. A recurring word in the speech was "partnership"—"a partnership guided by a healthy awareness that give and take is better than take it or leave it."

The major specific proposals of the speech centered on economic policy, and here Nixon stayed close to the line marked out by the Rockefeller report. The President promised to seek to implement the Rockefeller proposal for a general system of tariff preferences for all developing countries on the part of all developed countries, and to reduce non-tariff barriers to trade. He announced that he was ordering the "untying" of foreign aid—that is, allowing foreign aid dollars to be spent in other hemispheric countries as

---

[3]*Ibid.*, p. 144.

[4]Department of State publication 8501, Washington, D.C.: U.S. Government Printing Office (November 1969).

well as in the United States. He had already removed some other restrictions on the use of aid funds, and promised to re-examine those restrictions remaining. CIAP, the Inter-American Committee for the Alliance for Progress, which reviewed and made recommendations on the economic policies of the countries that received Alliance for Progress funds, would also be asked to review the economic policies of the United States.

On political questions, Mr. Nixon expressed strong hopes for the growth of democracy in the hemisphere, but added that "on the diplomatic level, we must deal realistically with governments in the inter-American system as they are." The Rockefeller proposal for a special Secretary for Western Hemisphere Affairs was modified to the raising of the rank of the Assistant Secretary of State for Inter-American Affairs to Under-Secretary, a proposal that Nixon undertook to submit to Congress, but which in fact engendered fierce opposition within the State Department and remained stillborn.

Although in itself the bulk of the speech was quite unexceptionable and contained a great deal of common sense, it did not come to grips with the three areas likely to present the most critical problems for the Nixon administration, the areas on which the Rockefeller report had been least helpful: what to do about the expropriation of U.S. property, whether to continue encouraging the military in a political role on the premise that their orientation would be "progressive," and the need to examine more carefully the actual scope and character of the "Communist menace" in the hemisphere. The Latin American military were not mentioned in the speech. Four sentences were devoted to the danger of armed subversion sponsored by one nation on another's territory. And the President spoke in general terms of the need to encourage private investment in Latin America, both domestic investment and that originating in the United States.

In some ways, the position on Latin American questions represented by the speech constituted a substantial step forward and reflected learning from past experience. A constructive position was taken on questions of international trade, probably the most important single determinant of the day-to-day economic and political health of the Latin American countries. Yet in this respect, as in others, the advice of Attorney General Mitchell, given in another context, seemed apropos: "Watch what we do, not what we say." During periods of economic difficulty, such as the one coinciding with Nixon's term of office, United States producers typically attempt to keep dwindling domestic markets for themselves by pushing for the exclusion of foreign products, trying to restrict international trade in a "beggar my neighbor" approach that provokes retaliation and ends by leaving everyone worse off than before. Pressures of this type built up during 1970, and in many of his legislative and administrative initiatives, Nixon yielded to them.

Tariffs and other obstacles continued to be placed on the importation of manufactured goods from Latin America (such as Brazilian-made instant coffee) where these competed with goods produced by influential U.S. firms. Latin Americans were quick to point out the paradox that the United States professed to support the economic development of Latin America, yet attempted to impede that development when it occurred. To the Latin Americans, the Nixon administration, like its predecessors, seemed noble and visionary in its general statements of policy but petty and short-sighted on concrete economic questions.

It was not long before major tests of the Nixon administration's approach to Latin America were posed in the three problem areas where the recommendations of the Rockefeller report and Nixon's own policy statements were especially deficient: the expropriation of U.S. property, governments run by the "progressive military," and the "Communist threat."

Shortly before Nixon took office, a military *coup* in Peru brought to power a group of officers of nationalist and quasi-socialist orientation. Their first major act once in power was to expropriate without compensation the holdings of the International Petroleum Company, a subsidiary of Standard Oil of New Jersey, and indeed opposition to the way in which the IPC problem had been handled by the incumbent president was one of the major factors leading to his removal by the *coup.* The case was an extremely complex one,[5] but there seem to have been strong arguments in favor of the Peruvian position that the IPC had benefited from an unduly favorable tax status over a long period of time. The Nixon administration took the position that under the terms of the Hickenlooper Amendment to the Foreign Assistance Act it had no choice but to discontinue economic aid to Peru unless adequate compensation was paid to the IPC, and reductions of purchases of sugar from Peru at the U.S. premium price were also hinted at. When the Peruvian government, with the enthusiastic support of all segments of Peruvian society, refused to yield its position, the United States finally let the threat to retaliate lapse, using a loophole clause in the amendment that allowed aid to continue while discussions leading to compensation were taking place—whereas in fact the only discussions of the matter had consisted of the Peruvians' negative responses to State Department requests for compensation for the company.

Thus on the problem of how to respond to the expropriation of U.S. property, on which the voluminous Rockefeller report had remained silent, the Nixon administration remained for some time at sea, while Governor Rockefeller's "progressive military" seemed to come into conflict with the United States precisely to the extent that they were in fact progressive. The

----

[5]See Richard Goodwin, "Letter from Peru," *The New Yorker* (May 17, 1969).

problem was finally resolved when the strongly pro-business Texan, John Connally, joined the Nixon Cabinet as Secretary of the Treasury, emerging in short order as the administration's "strong man" on economic questions. At Connally's prompting, and over State Department objections, the Export-Import Bank refused to finance the purchase by Chile of American passenger planes because the Chileans had nationalized U.S.-owned copper mines, even before compensation terms for the mines had been arrived at, and despite the fact that the Chilean government was trying valiantly to maintain good relations with the United States, against considerable pressure in the opposite direction. The denial of financing was supposed to act as a "deterrent" to other states' nationalizing United States property; in other words, it was based on precisely the same crude carrot-and-stick behavioralism that had again and again proved counter-productive in Latin America (see Chapter 7).

The other policy area in which the Nixon administration faced critical decisions—"the Communist threat"—was the area in which Governor Rockefeller had offered the poorest advice. With respect to the Soviet Union, Nixon had said some statesmanlike things about an era of confrontation giving way to an era of negotiations, and he initiated a détente with China; with respect to Communism in the hemisphere, however, all that the administration appeared to offer was a lack of information, understanding, and analytic capacity.

As in so many areas of foreign policy under the Nixon administration, difficulties arose not only from the predilections of the President himself but also from the distinctive character of the mind of his alter ego on foreign policy questions, Henry Kissinger, whose workings illustrated the paradox that profundity and superficiality are not necessarily mutually exclusive. The critical problem that raised the question of "Communism in the hemisphere" during the Nixon presidency was the election as Chile's president of Salvador Allende, representing a coalition that included the Communist party of Chile.

The contribution of Dr. Kissinger to the clarification of the issue consisted of a news briefing in Chicago in September 1970, after the popular election had taken place but before Allende's election had been confirmed by the Chilean Congress, which, according to newspaper reports, made the following points: "It was fairly easy to predict that if Dr. Salvador Allende was elected president of Chile by Congress on October 24, a Communist government would emerge in Chile. Argentina, Bolivia and Peru might follow Chile in forming Communist governments."[6] Kissinger was positing here a Latin American version of the "domino" theory, that venerable confusion of

---

[6]"Briefing on Chile Disturbs Latins" by Tad Szulc, *The New York Times* (September 23, 1970). Typographical errors in the original corrected. Dr. Kissinger was identified as the source of the briefing in subsequent reports, but not in the *Times* story.

geography and political science, which substitutes the perception of contiguity for the appreciation of causality and had long supplied the lack of intelligent thought about the problems of Southeast Asia. Anyone familiar with the processes of Argentine politics, with Argentine contempt for neighboring countries, or with the traditional frictions between Chile and Argentina over border and other issues, would find it more likely that if Argentina responded to events in Chile at all it would be by opposing them rather than by being influenced by them. Someone not familiar with these matters may catch a little of the flavor of Kissinger's views by comparing it to the analogous "if a socialist takes office in Mexico, then a Communist government will emerge there, and then the United States and Canada might form Communist governments too."

Dr. Kissinger's misunderstanding of the situation becomes less surprising, though not less shocking, if one gets an idea of the sort of information he was given by the intelligence reports he was reading.

In *The New York Times* of December 7, 1970, a front page story by Benjamin Welles, entitled "Soviet Intelligence Role in Latin America Rises," relayed the appreciation of the "Communist threat" held by "United States intelligence specialists."

It is perhaps worth examining this article at some length, since it appears representative of the sort of intelligence analysis which, bearing the prestigious CIA seal of approval, heavily influences those who make policy decisions for the United States.

Along with statistics on the number of Russian spies in Latin America and fascinating items of information such as that Soviet agents in Latin America no longer wore baggy pants and were often fluent in Spanish, the article contained a confused and inaccurate account of Russian relations with Cuba. At the same time, it failed to distinguish among Soviet intelligence activities, formal diplomatic relations between the Soviet government and Latin American governments, international trade relations, and domestic political alignments. The general quality of the analysis, which illustrates the fact that in the lexicon of Washington "intelligence" is not the opposite of stupidity, can be appreciated by the discussion of Soviet trade with the Latin American countries.

> Significantly, the analysts report, 3/4 of the trade is concentrated in two countries with strong, right-wing military governments—Brazil and Argentina. The remaining 1/4 is divided among all the other hemisphere countries, where, the analysts note, Moscow concentrates on buying commodities such as coffee, whose sales—and price—often balance the budgets of such states as Ecuador, Colombia, and Costa Rica.

The intelligence experts are not explicit about the portentous signifi-cance of the concentration of Soviet trade on Brazil and Argentina, so perhaps one is at liberty to think that it is because these countries do more trading abroad than the others. The diabolic Muscovite concentration on buying coffee from Colombia and Costa Rica may be, the layman might guess, because coffee is what Colombia and Costa Rica export and what the Soviet Union does not itself produce. What the Colombians and Costa Ricans don't appreciate, but which is hinted at by the article, is that since the last peso that balances the budget is not a dollar but a ruble, so to speak, the Soviet Union is given a critical influence on the national economy, which can then be used for political blackmail. (Of course, one's accounting has to be sophisticated to know which of the pesos earned by foreign sales is the one that actually balances the budget and therefore which foreign country should be allowed to exert a critical influence on your policies.)

Of especial importance in the context of the Nixon administration's predicament was the way "United States intelligence specialists" understood the situation in Chile.

> In Dr. Allende's cabinet, analysts note, socialists—some of whom are more extreme in Chile than the Communists—now hold such policy posts as the Foreign Ministry, the Interior Ministry, with control of the police, and the key position of secretary general of the government. Chilean Communists, by contrast, hold the patronage ministries of finance, labor and social welfare, public works, education and mines.

This is cited as proof that "Soviet and Cuban influence is reported to be rising in Chile." Let us take a look at the actual composition of Allende's cabinet to see what it shows of Communist influence—not of "Cuban and Soviet influence," which is a metaphysical concept applied to Chile. Allende's original cabinet was formed by a coalition of three large parties, together with some small ones and some independents. The three large parties were Allende's own Socialist party, the Communists, and the Radicals, a non-Marxist middle-class party of the center. Coalitions of these parties had held power before in Chile, it might be noted, in the 1930's and 1940's, at that time under Radical leadership.

Not including the position of secretary general of the cabinet, there were fourteen cabinet positions, three of which were assigned to each of the major parties. The Communists were assigned the portfolios of finance, labor, and public works, three of the politically least sensitive positions. They did not receive the ministries of mines and education, as Welles's story reported[7];

---

[7]The error was apparently that of Welles, not of his sources. Personal communication of Benjamin Welles to the author, March 3, 1971.

those portfolios, along with that of defense, went to the middle-class Radical party. The education ministry doubtless went to the Radicals since one of the party's main bases of support was in the country's high school teachers. The fact that the Radicals, the most conservative party in the coalition, were given the ministries of defense and mining constituted a clear indication of President Allende's attempt to reassure the military services and the foreign mining interests, the major industry scheduled for nationalization, that his government would not follow an irresponsible revolutionary line. Reserving of the cabinet secretariat and the foreign and interior ministries (along with the housing ministry) to the President's own party, the Socialists, indicated Allende's intention of maintaining close control of policy in those sensitive areas himself, rather than running the risk that they might get out of hand. In other words, the conclusions drawn by Welles's sources from the distribution of cabinet seats were diametrically opposed to the appropriate ones.

Not only the distribution of cabinet seats, but all of Allende's statements and actions, both since the presidential election and throughout a long political career, made clear that while a committed socialist, he was also a committed democrat. He made no secret of his solidarity with Fidel Castro's government in Cuba; but there was no "Cuban influence" on the Allende government, in the sense that because of Cuban wishes the government did anything it did not want to do, or would not have done if Fidel Castro had never been born. In fact, the influence went the other way, and after Allende's victory Castro had to acknowledge that violence was not always necessary to bring about the triumph of socialism in Latin America.

It is possible that "Soviet influence," hitherto small, might in the future grow in Chile, developing out of closer economic and technical relations. This is especially the case if the United States takes a hostile position toward the Chilean government. Thus the Chilean airline preferred to buy U.S.-made planes; but, when the Export-Import Bank refused to finance their purchase, the only alternative plane suitable was the Soviet-made Ilyushin, which the Russians made available on attractive credit terms.

Presumably "the intelligence community" was not likely to give a detailed briefing to a *New York Times* reporter without considerable forethought. One has to assume that the whole exercise was designed to show the Soviet Union how carefully U.S. intelligence kept track of its activities and to demonstrate the competence of the intelligence community to Washington and to the American public. The realization that the President and his advisor for National Security Affairs would be better informed and more understanding of events in Latin America if they subscribed to a good newspaper from the area[8] rather than reading "intelligence" reports is hardly

---

[8]After writing the above, the author came across a similar comment by Zbigniew Brzezinski:

comforting. But it may help to explain a lot about the quality of United States policy.

In sum, the Nixon policies toward Latin America were an inchoate mixture of sporadic common sense, misunderstanding, stereotyped thinking, lack of interest, and susceptibility to business pressure. The most dangerous ingredients in the mixture, given the actual political situation in most of the Latin American countries, were ideological anti-Communism and commitment to "protect" American investments. Fortunately for the Latin Americans and for the long-term interests of the United States in the area, it so happened that the countries where leftist-nationalist governments raised the anti-Communist and expropriation issues—Peru, Bolivia, and Chile—were all located in the area of South America furthest from the United States, out of the traditional Caribbean sphere of influence in which direct military intervention could reasonably be contemplated.

However, the Nixon administration should receive credit for acting with forethought to avoid its own Caribbean crisis. Under American prompting, transitional arrangements were made before François Duvalier's death which avoided a succession crisis and passed power smoothly to the dictator's son, Jean-Claude. Of course, Haiti remained an unsavory dictatorship, and the inevitable explosion was merely postponed. From Nixon's point of view, however, that result had to be considered a success. Eisenhower had intervened in Guatemala, Kennedy in Cuba, Johnson in the Dominican Republic. In the low state to which U.S.-Latin American relations had fallen, it had to be accounted an achievement of a kind that Nixon did not order troops into a Latin American country.

The lack of a clearly defined Latin American policy, or even of any real interest in the area, made the Nixon era a period of drift in inter-American relations, an interlude of marking time preparatory to the resumption of forward motion.

This writer can state on the basis of personal experience while serving in the Department of State that in most cases a better or at least as good a picture of foreign developments can be obtained by reading the better newspapers—including, of course, the foreign ones—than by perusing the hundreds of daily telegrams, often reporting cocktail-party trivia.

Between Two Ages: America's Role in the Technetronic Era, New York: Viking, 1970, p. 292, footnote.

11

In Conclusion

Practitioners of foreign policy are forever complaining that the work of academics is of no direct help to them as they go about their business. In reality this complaint is unsound. There is in fact a considerable body of theory about U.S. foreign policy that implies recommendations as to future courses of action. Yet even in cases in which the verdict of academic commentators is clear and virtually unanimous, this still appears not to influence the acts of policy-makers. For an academic audience, Thomas Mann can quote academics such as Arthur Whitaker and Howard Cline to the effect that military intervention in the Caribbean by the United States has always had counter-productive long-term results,[1] but this does not prevent him from urging a new military intervention the first time a difficult situation arises. And so it is with a certain sense of frustration that the writer attempts to make policy recommendations.

Because U.S. policies in the hemisphere have so often met with frustration, and have indeed so often proved to be counter-productive, it is tempting to move in the direction of a completely passive attitude, to the abnegation of an active role. This approach perhaps constitutes the United States' "second best" policy for Latin America and is certainly preferable to vigorous movement in the wrong direction. As a long-term proposition,

---

[1]Speech at Notre Dame, reproduced in the Appendix, pp. 145-153.

however, such a passive role is simply not viable. This has been shown most clearly on the question of recognition of new governments, where the United States has never been able to maintain for long the policy of automatic recognition which has often been attempted. The fact of the matter is that the United States is clearly the hegemonic power in the hemisphere, and cannot escape from this role. Its economic policies are of critical importance for Latin American governments, and even its political acts of only symbolic significance provide strong cues for action. In this respect, there is no possibility of a return to innocence. Since our acts necessarily have effects in the hemisphere, there is no responsible alternative to acting with consciousness of those effects, that is, to developing policies deliberately designed to achieve specific results.

In making recommendations for such policies, we continue to assume that the principal goals of the United States in the hemisphere are to assure national security, to promote national economic advantage, and to encourage the development of governments sympathetic to that of the United States and based on similar political principles.

NATIONAL SECURITY

For the United States, authentic national security problems in Latin America are in reality rather minor. Indeed, that is why the leading policy-makers generally ignore the area. Yet precisely because the United States has become accustomed to such a high degree of undisturbed security in the hemisphere, we tend to exaggerate the most marginal threat to that security, and to imagine threats when none exist. If we have learned anything from the experience of Vietnam, however, it is the likelihood, the danger, and the costliness of such overestimation of threats to national security. As Hecate told the witches in Macbeth,

> And you all know security
> Is mortals' chiefest enemy.

It is because of concern over national security that the United States has intervened with military force in recent years to attempt to remove unfriendly governments or to prevent such governments from taking power. Yet many states less powerful than the United States manage to survive with unfriendly neighbors, after all. At the same time, the dominant economic position of the United States in the hemisphere creates powerful pressures for potentially antagonistic governments to reach a *modus vivendi*. And in any case the frequency with which governments traditionally change in the area makes it unlikely that a deep-seated hostility will have to be lived with for long. The formidable difficulties that the Cubans brought on their heads by taking a hostile position toward the United States constitute a clear warning to governments contemplating a similar line of policy; Salvador Allende's caution and determination not to break with the United States clearly show the influence of lessons learned from Cuba.

Fearing for the national security, Eisenhower intervened in Guatemala, Kennedy in Cuba, Johnson in the Dominican Republic. The Dominican intervention was in no way required by the national security and was completely counter-productive for the cause of democracy and even of human decency. Kennedy's Cuban intervention was a failure. Eisenhower's was unnecessary, both because no threat of any kind existed, and because the Arbenz government would in all likelihood have been overthrown in a military *coup* within a short period of time anyway. The attempt by the United States to hold back the natural evolution of events in Guatemala and the Dominican Republic has been continued by military and police elements of those countries in the form of wide-ranging campaigns of torture and assassination. What the interventions actually achieved was to cause the deaths of innocent people, to cripple the possibility of democratic evolution, and to intensify hostility to the United States: in other words, the interventions themselves contributed to a long-term weakening of this nation's security.

THE PROMOTION OF DEMOCRATIC GOVERNMENT

The promotion of democracy, another of the historical aims of the United States in Latin America, is justified as a preference of the American people in its own right; at the same time, it is supportive of the interests of national security since, as history has demonstrated since the days of the Peloponnesian War, governments based on similar political principles are more likely to have friendly and cooperative relations with each other.

The promotion of democracy must be understood today not in the sense of imposing from outside a specific institution or set of institutions, as it was often conceived of in the days of Taft, Wilson, or Theodore Roosevelt. An institution that performs one function in a developed constitutional democracy may have quite other functions in countries at other stages of development. As Robert Burr has put it, the United States must "devise a new and more flexible definition of democracy—instead of stressing form and procedure emphasize values and life styles."[2]

---

[2]Robert N. Burr, *Our Troubled Hemisphere: Perspectives on United States-Latin American Relations,* Washington, D.C.: The Brookings Institution, 1967, p. 153.

What this means in effect is, on the one hand, United States tolerance of practices and institutions which contribute to the process of democratic development, even though in themselves they may not be those characteristic of a fully developed constitutional democracy—such as a transitional dominant one-party system of the Mexican type (assuming it is indeed transitional), or a spoils system for public-sector jobs where the government party is dedicated to reform and career bureaucrats would be conservative obstructionists; and, on the other hand, the ability and willingness to see beyond a carefully maintained façade of constitutional practice to an undemocratic authoritarian or oligarchic reality. Thus, although in principle effective government is a characteristic of a developed society, there is no merit, for example, in mounting AID programs to strengthen government instrumentalities when these are used by anti-democratic governments for purposes of repression, such as, let us say, the Brazilian police or the Dominican Army.

At the same time, the adoption of this developmental perspective means appreciation of the fact that while political development may, one hopes, lead ultimately to stable constitutional democracy, in the short run the extension of political participation that is one aspect of development means the posing of new mass demands and a higher order of political turbulence. If it is understood that this is an inevitable concomitant of the extension of participation in Latin America, just as it was during the last century in Britain, the Netherlands, and Scandinavia, and as it was and is in the United States, then there should be less of a tendency to interpret this turbulence as unnatural, or necessarily organized by hostile alien forces, or necessarily inimical to United States interests in stability and peaceful cooperation and calling for U.S. intervention of some kind.

Only in the imagination of Thomas Mann does an American policy of support for democracy in the hemisphere such as the one outlined here mean a policy of direct military intervention to overthrow governments and install new ones. This is a straw man of right-wing argument; historically U.S. military intervention in Latin America has typically taken place against the left, or on behalf of private economic interests. But there are many occasions on which acts of commission or omission on the part of United States representatives falling far short of military intervention will necessarily have the effect of strengthening one or another domestic political tendency. On such occasions the interest of the United States in the promotion of government that is democratic, responsible, popular, and progressive, rather than fear of change, desire to play it safe, or a rigid ideological distrust of "the left," should provide the cues for action.

Increasingly, governments coming to power in Latin America will reflect popular desires and aspirations. Whether the United States can maintain cooperative relations with the governments of the future will be affected by whether it has acted so as to promote or frustrate those aspirations.

ECONOMIC GOALS

One of the irreducible functions of a government is the protection of the property of its nationals abroad. Traditionally, the United States has accepted that a government may find it necessary or desirable to expropriate the property of United States nationals within its jurisdiction, but in such cases has insisted that "prompt, adequate, and effective" compensation be provided. The problems that such cases give rise to are likely to be much with us in the coming period, as the tide of nationalism in Latin America rises.

It is important to recognize that the circumstances of each case differ. There is not much cause for righteous indignation, for example, when it is a question of nationalizing an American company that has made extremely high profits on the basis of a law or contract that inadequately protected the interests of the country in which it was doing business, especially if, as sometimes occurs, the relevant law was adopted, or the property was acquired, under morally or legally dubious circumstances. Nevertheless, it does remain incumbent on the United States government to attempt to secure fair treatment for U.S. companies, whatever "fair treatment" may entail in a given case. The goal of U.S. representatives in such cases should be to reach a generally satisfactory solution that can be lived with, economically and politically, by all parties concerned, not to adopt the demands of the affected company as their own and defend them to the last ditch, as was done in the Peruvian IPC case. A reminder that the cause of economic growth is served by a climate that makes business confidence possible is more consistent with this approach than threats of retaliation. In such cases, it is likely that compromises will have to be made and it is well to appreciate that at the outset, rather than to become committed to a rigid position of principle from which it is difficult to compromise. In questions of this type, the *style* of policy is of critical importance.

What needs to be more appreciated by U.S. policy-makers is that there are economic interests of the United States *as a whole* vis-à-vis Latin America over and above the defense of specific private economic interests. Principal among these is the expansion of trade. The primary immediate and direct beneficiary of private investment is the investor, and investment carries with it political problems such as the fact that decisions affecting a large segment of the national economy may be made exclusively by foreigners consulting only their own economic interests. The expansion of trade, on the other hand—though not free from political problems—brings benefits more generally distributed among all concerned.

Despite the general desirability of trade expansion, however, there are specific private interests that stand to benefit, at least in the short run, from the restriction of international trade, so that the cause of trade expansion needs always to be vigorously fought for. The rigidities and vagaries of the international payments situation, coupled with the economically restrictive measures that states believe themselves forced to take under the influence of payments difficulties, present real dangers here. Thus the forces of economic nationalism, protection, and autarchy are strengthened and encouraged by problems that arise commonly in national balances of payments, and strenuous efforts are necessary if the world economy is not to be shrunk in a new era of economic restrictionism.

In Latin America the problem is especially delicate. The two ideological approaches to world trade—economic liberalism, or free trade, and economic nationalism, or the concentration on building domestic industry behind a tariff wall—have acquired significance as rival political positions within most countries. The forces of economic nationalism are particularly strong, being able to depict their position as "patriotic' and attacking the economic liberals as *entreguistas,* or those who would sell out to foreigners.

From the viewpoint of the national interest of each country, the policies of either camp have substantial drawbacks. The policy of the economic nationalists, who wish to reduce the buying of foreign goods and develop a domestic manufacturing industry behind a protective tariff, leads typically to the creation of a high-priced and inefficient industry, hurting the consumer and holding back the growth of the total national product, although a limited sector does improve its relative economic position. This point is widely appreciated and its truth has been documented in several cases.[3]

The dangers of a policy of complete economic liberalism are also significant. Complete integration into the world economy means that the national economy may be subject to excessive fluctuations in response to world market conditions; if a regime of completely free monetary exchange exists, the resultant instability in the value of the national currency may make rational planning and development, public or private, difficult and thus work against the interests of growth. At the same time, the requirements of

---

[3]For discussion of the stagnation of the economically nationalist Argentine and Uruguayan economies, see Herman E. Daly, "The Uruguayan Economy: Its Basic Nature and Current Problems," *Journal of Inter-American Studies,* 7, 3 (July 1965), and Carlos Díaz-Alejandro, "An Interpretation of Argentine Economic Growth since 1930," *Journal of Development Studies,* 3, 1 and 2 (October 1966) and (January 1967).

the international division of labor may indicate a concentration on agriculture and extractive industry at the same time as an irreversible tendency to urbanization creates a work force that can no longer be employed in the primary sector.

Under the present circumstances, a policy based on either ideological extreme is likely to have unfortunate results. What the countries of the area need instead is an economic policy that aims at trade expansion but still increases the number of productive jobs in urban areas and minimizes the excessive instability that results from complete reliance on the world market. The Central American common market and the Andean regional grouping represent moves in the direction of this type of mixed economic policy, combining stimuli to the growth of manufacturing with trade expansion. Both efforts should have the firm and consistent support of the United States.

In this context, the major danger to the economic well-being of Latin America that grows out of United States policy is not the reduction in amounts of aid committed, which may be a more visible public issue—the impact of "aid" is generally overrated—but is the possibility of a strong movement toward economic protectionism. The germs of that virus are always with us, awaiting a time when the body is weak and unable to resist them. Such a time is unfortunately upon us today and a host of special interests have been importuning the Congress to legislate ways of putting into their pockets money taken from foreign producers and American consumers. The arguments that are made on behalf of these special interests should not make us lose sight of the fact that growth in the economic welfare and political stability of *all* the countries of the world, including the United States, depends on the steady expansion of world trade.[4]

---

[4]The self-defeating shortsightedness of restrictions on trade that grow out of concern for balance-of-payments problems can be illustrated very simply by developments on the United States-Mexican border in early 1968. Concerned about the outflow of gold and dollars, President Johnson had the value of duty-free goods that could be brought in to the United States by returning travelers reduced to $100 and the amount of duty-free liquor that could be brought back reduced from one gallon to one quart. This had the effect of severely damaging trade along the Mexican side of the border, causing economic loss and unemployment. However, it also had an adverse effect on Mexico's balance of payments, and the Mexican government thereupon decided to reduce the outflow of pesos by more stringent enforcement of the rules governing the bringing back to the country of purchases from the United States. As a result, substantial economic damage was done to the many businesses on the United States' side of the border making retail sales to visiting residents of Mexico. The net result of this sequence of events was that the amount spent by Mexicans in the United States was reduced by about the same amount Americans spent in Mexico, leaving the United States-Mexico balance of payments about where it was originally but at a lower level of total trade; but meanwhile economic

IN SUMMARY

North Americans often worry if the Latin Americans are "on our side." Yet it would be more to the point for us to ask ourselves if we are on their side. We need to understand that the long-term national interests and aspirations of the United States can be brought into harmony with the interests of the peoples of Latin America—that is, they can if we can divest ourselves of a narrow preoccupation with the private interests of individual economic groupings, with shibboleths about national security that shroud a failure to understand concrete present-day conditions, or with the ideological fixations left over from the last generation but one.

If we clear irrelevant clutter from our heads and our policies, perhaps we will be able to perceive the revolutionary forces at work in Latin America today; and then we might be able to see that intelligent policies for the promotion of political, as well as economic, development can work with these forces and not against them, to produce results that are consonant with U.S. national interests and that at the same time express the values that most Americans, and most Latin Americans, share.

---

hardship had been imposed on people on both sides of the border. The deleterious effects of economic restrictionism are not always so directly and immediately apparent as in the case cited, but they occur nevertheless.

Selected Bibliography

I. U.S. Policy Toward Latin America, General

Bemis, Samuel F. *The Latin-American Policy of the United States.* New York: W. W. Norton, 1967. (Originally published by Harcourt Brace in 1943.)

Burr, Robert N. *Our Troubled Hemisphere: Perspectives on United States-Latin American Relations.* Washington, D.C.: Brookings Institute, 1967.

Dreier, John C. *The Organization of American States and the Hemisphere Crisis.* New York: Harper & Row, 1962.

Fulbright, William J. *The Arrogance of Power.* New York: Random House (Vintage), 1967.

Hammond, Paul Y. "Presidents, Politics, and Intervention," *The Annals* (November 1969).

Hoffman, Stanley. "The American Style: Our Past and Our Principles," *Foreign Affairs* (January 1968).

Levin, N. Gordon, Jr. *Woodrow Wilson and World Politics: America's Response to War and Revolution.* New York: Oxford University Press, 1968.

Mecham, J. Lloyd. *The United States and Inter-American Security, 1889-1960.* Austin, Texas: University of Texas Press, 1961.

Morris, Bernard S. *International Communism and American Foreign Policy.* New York: Atherton Press, 1966.

Munro, Dana G. *Intervention and Dollar Diplomacy in the Caribbean, 1900-1921.* Princeton, N.J.: Princeton University Press, 1964.

Needler, Martin C. *Understanding Foreign Policy.* New York: Holt, Rinehart & Winston, 1966.

Perkins, Dexter. *A History of the Monroe Doctrine* (Rev. ed.) Boston: Little, Brown, 1955.

_____ . *The American Approach to Foreign Policy.* (Rev. ed.) Cambridge, Mass.: Harvard University Press, 1962.

Plank, John (Ed.) *Cuba and the United States: Long Range Perspectives.* Washington, D.C.: Brookings Institute, 1967.

Pratt, Julius W. *America's Colonial Experiment.* Englewood Cliffs, N.J.: Prentice-Hall, 1950.

Ronning, C. Neale. *Law and Politics in Inter-American Diplomacy.* New York: Wiley, 1963.

Rosenau, James N. (Ed.) *Domestic Sources of Foreign Policy.* New York: Free Press, 1967.

Schlesinger, Arthur M., Jr. *A Thousand Days.* Boston: Houghton Mifflin, 1965. (Fawcett paperback edition, 1967).

_____ . "Origins of the Cold War," *Foreign Affairs* (October 1967).

Tannenbaum, Frank. *The American Tradition in Foreign Policy.* Norman, Okla.: University of Oklahoma Press, 1955.

Thomas, A. V. W., and Thomas, A. J., Jr. *The Organization of American States.* Dallas, Texas: Southern Methodist University Press, 1963.

Tulchin, Joseph S. "Inhibitions Affecting the Formulation and Execution of the Latin American Policy of the United States," *Ventures* (Fall 1967).

Windmiller, Marshall. "Toward a Value Maximizing Foreign Policy," paper delivered at American Political Science Association annual meeting (September 1969) (mimeo).

Wolf, Charles, Jr. *United States Policy and the Third World.* Boston: Little, Brown, 1967.

Wood, Bryce. *The Making of the Good Neighbor Policy.* New York: Columbia University Press, 1961.

II. Political and Social Development

Adams, Richard, et al. *Social Change in Latin America Today.* New York: Random House, 1960.

Finkle, Jason, and Gable, Richard (Eds.) *Political Development and Social Change.* New York: Wiley, 1967.

Germani, Gino. *Política y sociedad en una época de transición.* Buenos Aires: Editorial Paidos, 1964.

Heath, Dwight B., and Adams, Richard N. (Eds.) *Contemporary Cultures and Societies of Latin America.* New York: Random House, 1965.

Johnson, John J. (Ed.) *Continuity and Change in Latin America.* Stanford, Calif.: Stanford University Press, 1964.

Lambert, Jacques. *Latin America: Social Structures and Political Institutions.* Berkeley and Los Angeles: University of California Press, 1967.

Lipset, Seymour M., and Solari, Aldo E. (Eds.) *Elites in Latin America.* New York: Oxford University Press, 1967.

Needler, Martin C. *Political Development in Latin America: Instability, Violence, and Evolutionary Change.* New York: Random House, 1968.

Pye, Lucian. "The Concept of Political Development," *The Annals* (March 1965).

——————. *Aspects of Political Development.* Boston: Little, Brown, 1966.

Riggs, Fred W. "The Theory of Political Development," in James C. Charlesworth (Ed.), *Contemporary Political Analysis,* New York: The Free Press, 1967.

Snow, Peter (Ed.) *Government and Politics in Latin America.* New York: Holt, Rinehart & Winston, 1967.

Veliz, Claudio (Ed.) *Obstacles to Change in Latin America.* New York: Oxford University Press, 1965.

III. Economic Development and U.S. Aid

Anderson, Charles W. *Politics and Economic Change in Latin America.* Princeton, N.J.: Van Nostrand, 1967.

Binning, William C. "The Nixon Foreign Aid Policy to Latin America," *Inter-American Economic Affairs* (June 1971).

Brzezinski, Z. "The Politics of Underdevelopment," *World Politics* (October 1956).

Department of Economic Affairs, Pan American Union. *Problems and Perspectives of Economic Development: 1963-64.* Baltimore: Johns Hopkins University Press, 1966.

Engler, Robert. *The Politics of Oil.* New York: Macmillan, 1961.

Fillol, Tomás Roberto. *Social Factors in Economic Development: The Argentine Case.* Cambridge, Mass.: MIT Press, 1961.

Gordon, Lincoln. *A New Deal for Latin America: The Alliance for Progress.* Cambridge, Mass.: Harvard University Press, 1963.

Groves, Roderick T. "Expropriation in Latin America: Some Observations," *Inter-American Economic Affairs* (December 1969).

Hanson, Simon G. *Dollar Diplomacy Modern Style: Chapters in the Failure of the Alliance for Progress.* Washington, D.C.: Inter-American Affairs Press, 1970.

Hirschman, Albert O. *The Strategy of Economic Development.* New Haven, Conn.: Yale University Press, 1958.

_____. (Ed.) *Latin American Issues: Essays and Comments.* New York: Twentieth Century Fund, 1961.

_____. *Journeys Toward Progress.* New York: Twentieth Century Fund, 1963.

Johnson, Harry G. *Economic Policies Toward Less Developed Countries.* Washington, D.C.: Brookings Institute, 1967.

Mason, Edward S. *Foreign Aid and Foreign Policy.* New York: Harper & Row, 1964.

Mikesell, Raymond F. *The Economics of Foreign Aid.* Chicago: Aldine, 1968.

Model, Leo. "The Politics of Private Foreign Investment," *Foreign Affairs* (July 1967).

Montgomery, John D. *The Politics of Foreign Aid.* New York: Praeger, 1962.

Packenham, Robert A. "Political Development Doctrines in the American Foreign Aid Program," *World Politics* (January 1966).

Pearse, Andrew. "Agrarian Change Trends in Latin America," *Latin American Research Review* (Summer 1966).

Rosenstein-Rodan, P.N. "International Aid for Underdeveloped Countries," *The Review of Economics and Statistics* (May 1961).

Schaedel, Richard P. "Land Reform Studies," *Latin American Research Review* (Fall 1965).

Staley, Eugene. *The Future of Underdeveloped Countries.* New York: Praeger, 1961.

Urquidi, Víctor. *The Challenge of Development in Latin America.* New York: Praeger, 1961.

Weintraub, Sidney. *Trade Preferences for Less-Developed Countries: An Analysis of U.S. Policy.* New York: Praeger, 1967.

White, Gillian. *Nationalization and Foreign Property.* New York: Praeger, 1961.

Wiggins, James W., and Schoek, Helmut (Eds.) *Foreign Aid Re-Examined: A Critical Appraisal.* Washington, D.C.: Public Affairs Press, 1958.

Wolf, Charles, Jr. "The Political Effects of Economic Programs: Some Indicators from Latin America," *Economic Development and Cultural Change* (October 1965).

IV. The Latin American Military

Adams, Richard N. "The Development of the Guatemalan Military," *Studies in Comparative International Development,* 4, 5 (1968-1969).

Alba, Víctor. *El militarismo.* Mexico: Editorial Cultura, 1960.

——————— . "The Stages of Militarism in Latin America," in John J. Johnson (Ed.), *The Role of the Military in Underdeveloped Countries.* Princeton, N.J.: Princeton University Press, 1962.

Astiz, Carlos Alberto. "The Peruvian Armed Forces as a Political Elite: Can They Develop a New Developmental Model?" paper delivered at International Political Science Association Round Table, Rio de Janeiro (October 1969) (mimeo).

Bañales G., Carlos. "Las fuerzas armadas en la crisis uruguaya," *Aportes* (July 1968).

Barber, Willard F., and Ronning, C. Neale. *Internal Security and Military Power: Counterinsurgency and Civic Action in Latin America.* Columbus: Ohio State University Press, 1966.

Bienen, Henry (Ed.), *The Military Intervenes: Case Studies in Political Development.* New York: Russell Sage Foundation, 1968.

Brill, William H. *Military Intervention in Bolivia: The Overthrow of Paz Estenssoro and the MNR.* Washington, D.C.: Institute for the Comparative Study of Political Systems, 1967.

Canton, Darío. "Notas sobre las fuerzas armadas argentinas," *Revista Latinoamericana de Sociología* (November 1965).

_____ . "Military Intervention in Argentina: 1900-1966," Documento de Trabajo 39, Buenos Aires: Centro de Investigaciones Sociales, Instituto Torcuato di Tella, 1967.

Cuéllar, Oscar. "Notas sobre la participación política de los militares en América Latina," *Aportes* (January 1971).

Dean, Warren. "Latin American Golpes and Economic Fluctuations, 1823-1966," *Social Science Quarterly* (June 1970).

Díez de Medina, G. Mario. "Los nasseristas de Bolivia," *Temas Sociales* (March 1970).

Einaudi, Luigi. *The Peruvian Military: A Summary Political Analysis.* RAND Memorandum RM-6048-RC (May 1969).

_____ . *Peruvian Military Relations with the United States.* RAND P-4389 (June 1970).

Estrategia. Special issue on the armed forces in Latin American politics (July-August 1969).

Finer, S. E. *The Man on Horseback.* New York: Praeger, 1963.

Fitzgibbon, Russell H. "What Price Latin American Armies?" *Virginia Quarterly Review* (Autumn 1960).

Germani, Gino, and Silvert, Kalman H. "Politics, Social Structure, and Military Intervention in Latin America," *European Journal of Sociology,* II (1961).

Goldwert, Marvin. "The Rise of Modern Militarism in Argentina," *Hispanic American Historical Review,* 48, 2 (May 1968).

Hansen, Roy A. "Military Culture and the Political Role of the Military in Chile," paper presented at American Sociological Association meeting (August 1968) (mimeo).

Horowitz, Irving L. "The Military Elite," in Seymour Lipset and Aldo Solari (Eds.), *Elites in Latin America,* New York: Oxford University Press, 1967.

Janowitz, Morris. *The Military in the Political Development of New Nations.* Chicago: University of Chicago Press, 1964.

Johnson, John J. (Ed.) *The Role of the Military in Underdeveloped Countries.* Princeton, N.J.: Princeton University Press, 1962.

_____ . *The Military and Society in Latin America.* Stanford, Calif.: Stanford University Press, 1964.

Lieuwen, Edwin. *Arms and Politics in Latin America.* (Rev. ed.) New York: Praeger, 1961.

——————. *Generals Vs. Presidents.* New York: Praeger, 1964.

——————. "The Military: A Force for Continuity or Change," in John TePaske and Sydney Fischer (Eds.), *Explosive Forces in Latin America,* Columbus: Ohio State University Press, 1964.

——————. "The Latin American Military and U.S. Policy," prepared for U.S. Senate Subcommittee on American Republics Affairs, Washington, D.C.: Government Printing Office (October 9, 1967).

——————. *Mexican Militarism.* Albuquerque, N.M.: University of New Mexico Press, 1969.

Loftus, Joseph E. *Latin American Defense Expenditures, 1938-1965.* RAND Memorandum RM-5310-PR/ISA (January 1968).

McAlister, Lyle. "Changing Concepts of the Role of the Military in Latin America," *The Annals* (July 1965).

——————. "Recent Research and Writings on the Role of the Military in Latin America," *Latin American Research Review* (Fall 1966).

——————, et. al. *The Military in Latin American Sociopolitical Evolution: Four Case Studies.* Washington, D.C.: Center for Research in Social Systems (January 1970).

Merkx, Gilbert W. "Legalidad, cambio político e impacto social en los cambios de presidentes latinoamericanos, 1930-1965," *Revista Latinoamericana de Sociología* (October 1968).

Miguens, José Enrique. "Una nueva metodología para el estudio de los golpes militares en Latinoamérica," *Estrategia* (July-August 1969).

Needler, Martin C. *Anatomy of a Coup d'Etat: Ecuador, 1963.* Washington, D.C.: Institute for the Comparative Study of Political Systems, 1964.

——————. "Political Development and Military Intervention in Latin America," *American Political Science Review* (September 1966).

——————. "The Latin American Military: Predatory Reactionaries or Modernizing Patriots?" *Journal of Inter-American Studies* (April 1969).

Payne, Arnold. *The Peruvian Coup d'Etat of 1962: The Overthrow of Manuel Prado.* Washington, D.C.: Institute for the Comparative Study of Political Systems, 1968.

Payne, James. "Peru: The Politics of Structured Violence," *Journal of Politics* (August 1965).

Potash, Robert A. *The Army and Politics in Argentina 1928-1945: Yrigoyen to Perón.* Stanford, Calif.: Stanford University Press, 1969.

Putnam, Robert D. "Toward Explaining Military Intervention in Latin American Politics," *World Politics* (October 1967).

Saint Jean, Ibérico Manuel. "Los ejércitos de Argentina y Brasil: algunos aspectos comparativos," *Estrategia* (January-February 1970).

Solaún, Mauricio. *Sociologia de los golpes de estado latino americanos.* Bogotá: Universidad de los Andes, 1969.

Taylor, Philip B., Jr. *The Venezuelan Golpe de Estado de 1958: The Fall of Marcos Pérez Jiménez.* Washington, D.C.: Institute for the Comparative Study of Political Systems, 1968.

"United States Military Policies and Programs in Latin America," transcript of hearings before Senate subcommittee on Western Hemisphere Affairs, June 24 and July 8, 1969, Washington, D.C.: Government Printing Office, 1969.

Weaver, Jerry. "La élite política de un régimen dominado por militares: el ejemplo de Guatemala," *Revista Latinoamericana de Sociología,* **69**, 1 (March 1969).

Wilson, Desmond P., Jr., and Horack, Jessie. "Military Recruitment and Militarism in Latin America," prepared for President's Commission on an All-Volunteer Armed Force (September 12, 1969) (unpublished).

V. Cuba

Alexander, Robert J. *Communism in Latin America,* New Brunswick, N.J.: Rutgers University Press, 1957.

Blackburn, Robin. "Prologue to the Cuban Revolution," *New Left Review* (October 1963).

Bonachea, Rolando, and Valdés, Nelson (Eds.) *Che: Selected Works of Ernesto Guevara.* Cambridge, Mass.: MIT Press, 1970.

Castro, Fidel. *History Will Absolve Me.* New York: Lyle Stuart, 1961.

——————. "This Shame Will Be Welcome . . . ," speech of July 26, 1970, *The New York Review of Books* (September 24, 1970).

Chapman, Charles E. *A History of the Cuban Republic.* New York: Macmillan, 1927.

Clark, Joseph. "Thus Spake Fidel Castro," *Dissent* (January-February 1970).

"The Cuban Disaster," *Time* (April 28, 1961).

Draper, Theodore. *Castro's Revolution: Myths and Realities.* New York: Praeger, 1962.

——————. *Castroism: Theory and Practice.* New York: Praeger, 1965.

——————. "Five Years of Castro's Cuba," *Commentary* (January 1964).

Goldenberg, Boris. *The Cuban Revolution and Latin America.* London: Praeger, 1965.

Gray, Richard B. *José Martí: Cuban Patriot.* Gainesville: University of Florida Press, 1962.

Jenks, Leland. *Our Cuban Colony.* New York: Vanguard, 1928.

Larson, David L. (Ed.) *The "Cuban Crisis" of 1962: Selected Documents and Chronology.* Boston: Houghton Mifflin, 1963.

MacGaffey, Wyatt, and Barnett, Clifford R. *Cuba: Its People, Its Society, Its Culture.* New Haven, Conn.: Yale University Press, 1962.

Mañach, Jorge. *Martí: Apostle of Freedom.* New York: Devin-Adair, 1950.

Martz, John D. "Doctrine and Dilemmas of the Latin American 'New Left'," *World Politics* (January 1970).

Nelson, Lowry. *Rural Cuba.* Minneapolis: University of Minnesota Press, 1950.

Pachter, Henry M. *Collision Course: The Cuban Missile Crisis and Coexistence.* New York: Praeger, 1963.

Poppino, Rollie. *International Communism in Latin America.* New York: The Free Press of Glencoe, 1964.

Seers, Dudley, et al. *Cuba: The Economic and Social Revolution.* Chapel Hill: University of North Carolina Press, 1964.

Semidei, Manuela. *Les Etats-Unis et la révolution cubaine, 1959-1964.* Paris: Armand Colin, 1968.

Smith, Robert F. *The United States and Cuba: Business and Diplomacy, 1917-1960.* New York: Bookman Associates, 1960.

——————————.(Ed.) *Background to Revolution: The Development of Modern Cuba.* New York: Knopf, 1966.

Suárez, Andrés. *Cuba: Castroism and Communism, 1959-1966.* Cambridge, Mass.: MIT Press, 1967.

Szulc, Tad, and Meyer, Karl. *The Cuban Invasion.* New York: Praeger, 1962.

Thomas, Hugh. "Middle Class Politics and the Cuban Revolution," in Claudio Veliz (Ed.), *The Politics of Conformity,* London: Oxford University Press, 1967.

Valdés, Nelson. "La diplomacia del azúcar," *Aportes* (October 1970).

VI. The Dominican Republic

Bosch, Juan. "A Tale of Two Nations," *The New Leader* (June 21, 1965).

——————————. "Santo Domingo," *The New Republic* (July 24, 1965).

——————————. "Communism and Democracy in the Dominican Republic," *Saturday Review* (August 7, 1965).

——————————. *The Unfinished Experiment: Democracy in the Dominican Republic.* New York: Praeger, 1966.

Crassweller, Robert D. *Trujillo: The Life and Times of a Caribbean Dictator.* New York: Macmillan, 1966.

Draper, Theodore. "The Roots of the Dominican Crisis," *The New Leader* (May 24, 1965).

—————. "The Dominican Crisis: A Case Study in American Policy," *Commentary* (December 1965).

—————. "U.S. Intelligence Vs. Juan Bosch," *The New Republic* (February 19, 1966).

—————. "Defaming Bosch," *The New Republic* (February 26, 1966).

Estrella, Julio C. *La revolución dominicana y la crisis de la OEA,* published by the author, Santo Domingo, 1965.

Kurzman, Dan. *Santo Domingo: Revolt of the Damned.* New York: G. P. Putnam's Sons, 1965.

Lowenthal, Abraham F. "The Dominican Republic: The Politics of Chaos," in A. von Lazar and Robert R. Kaufman (Eds.), *Reform and Revolution: Readings in Latin American Politics,* Boston: Allyn and Bacon, 1969.

Mann, Thomas C. "The Democratic Ideal in Our Policy Toward Latin America," Commencement Address, University of Notre Dame, June 7, 1964 (Department of State Press Release No. 268, June 5, 1964).

—————. Address before the annual meeting of the Inter-American Press Association, San Diego, Calif., October 12, 1965 (Department of State Press Release No. 241, October 12, 1965).

Martin, John Bartlow. *Overtaken by Events: The Dominican Crisis from the Fall of Trujillo to the Civil War.* Garden City, N.Y.: Doubleday, 1966.

Osborne, William D. (Ed.) *The Dominican Republic: A Bilingual Report.* San Germán, Puerto Rico: Inter-American University Press, 1964.

Rodman, Selden. "A Close View of Santo Domingo," *The Reporter* (July 15, 1965).

Slater, Jerome. "The United States, the Organization of American States, and the Dominican Republic, 1961-1963," *International Organization,* **XVIII**, 2 (1964).

—————. "The Limits of Legitimization in International Organizations: The Organization of American States and the Dominican Crisis," *International Organization,* **XXIII**, 1 (1969).

Szulc, Tad. *Dominican Diary.* New York: Delacorte Press, 1965.

—————. "When the Marines Stormed Ashore in Santo Domingo," *Saturday Evening Post,* July 31, 1965.

Thomas, Norman (Ed.) *Dominican Republic: A Study in the New Imperialism.* New York: Institute for International Labor Research, n.d. (1965).

Welles, Summer. *Naboth's Vineyard.* 2 vols. New York: Payson and Clarke, 1928.

Wiarda, Howard J. *Materials for the Study of Politics and Government in the Dominican Republic, 1930-1966.* Santiago de los Caballeros, Dominican Republic: Asociación Para el Desarrollo Inc. and Universidad Católica "Madre y Maestra," 1967.

_____. *Dictatorship and Development: The Methods of Control in Trujillo's Dominican Republic.* Gainesville: University of Florida Press, 1968.

_____. *Dominican Republic: Nation in Transition.* New York: Praeger, 1969.

VII. Recognition of De Facto *Regimes*

Borchard, Edwin. "Recognition and Non-Recognition," *American Journal of International Law* (January 1942).

Brown, Philip M. "The Legal Effects of Recognition," *American Journal of International Law* (October 1950).

del Carril, Bonifacio. *Reconocimiento de los gobiernos de facto.* Buenos Aires: Ministerio de Relaciones Exteriores y Culto, 1962.

Goebel, Julius, Jr. *The Recognition Policy of the United States,* doctoral dissertation, Columbia University, 1915.

Hughes, Charles Evans. *Our Relations to the Nations of the Western Hemisphere.* Princeton, N.J.: Princeton University Press, 1928.

Lauterpacht, Hersh. *Recognition in International Law.* Cambridge, Mass.: Cambridge University Press, 1947.

Needler, Martin C. "United States Recognition Policy and the Peruvian Case," *Inter-American Economic Affairs* (Spring 1963).

Neumann, William A., Jr. *Recognition of Governments in the Americas.* Washington, D.C.: Foundation for Foreign Affairs, 1947.

Ronning, C. Neale. *Law and Politics in Inter-American Diplomacy.* New York: Wiley, 1963, Chap. 2.

Wright, Theodore P., Jr. *American Support of Free Elections Abroad.* Washington, D.C.: Public Affairs Press, 1964.

Appendix

Three Documents

The three documents which follow have been chosen to represent the orientations on Latin American questions of the three most recent administrations. It should be remembered that these three statements describe policies it was hoped to follow; they do not necessarily reflect the policies that were actually implemented.

The Charter of Punta del Este embodied the hope of the Kennedy administration that it would be possible, with the help of U.S. funds, to organize a coordinated effort to develop the Latin American countries economically, and at the same time socially and politically. As noted in the body of this book, the effort met with only limited success.

The Notre Dame speech of Assistant Secretary Mann, "The Democratic Ideal in Our Policy Toward Latin America," is a characteristic document of the Johnson administration. While paying lip-service to the democratic aspirations for the hemisphere of the Kennedy administration and most of its predecessors, some of the difficulties encountered by policies to promote democracy, either real or hypothetical, are adduced in ways which have the effect of blurring rather than clarifying the issues, and a proviso is introduced explicitly exempting cases of "Communism." The net effect is to provide justifications for military intervention and benevolent neutrality toward anti-democratic regimes on the part of the United States, in the guise of a policy of non-intervention and support of democracy.

President Nixon's speech, "Action for Progress for the Americas," is also a characteristic document. By conscious contrast with the dramatic initiatives of President Kennedy—"I offer no grandiose promises and no panaceas"—Nixon promises improvement of mutual relations on some minor points; the major promises, on trade preferences and the upgrading of the State Department officer dealing with Latin American questions, have, at the time of writing, yet to be implemented.

I

The Charter of Punta del Este

We, the American Republics, hereby proclaim our decision to unite in a common effort to bring our people accelerated economic progress and broader social justice within the framework of personal dignity and political liberty.

Almost two hundred years ago we began in this Hemisphere the long struggle for freedom which now inspires people in all parts of the world. Today, in ancient lands, men moved to hope by the revolutions of our young nations search for liberty. Now we must give a new meaning to that revolutionary heritage. For America stands at a turning point in history. The men and women of our Hemisphere are reaching for the better life which today's skills have placed within their grasp. They are determined for themselves and their children to have decent and ever more abundant lives, to gain access to knowledge and equal opportunity for all, to end those conditions which benefit the few at the expense of the needs and dignity of the many. It is our inescapable task to fulfill these just desires—to demonstrate to the poor and forsaken of our countries, and of all lands, that the creative powers of free men hold the key to their progress and to the progress of future generations. And our certainty of ultimate success rests not alone on our faith in ourselves and in our nations but on the indomitable spirit of free man which has been the heritage of American civilization.

Inspired by these principles, and by the principles of Operation Pan America and the Act of Bogotá, the American Republics hereby resolve to adopt the following program of action to establish and carry forward an Alliance for Progress.

TITLE I.   OBJECTIVES OF THE ALLIANCE FOR PROGRESS

It is the purpose of the Alliance for Progress to enlist the full energies of the peoples and governments of the American republics in a great cooperative effort to accelerate the economic and social development of the participating countries of Latin America, so that they may achieve maximum levels of well-being, with equal opportunities for all, in democratic societies adapted to their own needs and desires.

The American republics agree to work toward the achievement of the following fundamental goals in the present decade:

1. To achieve in the participating Latin American countries a substantial and sustained growth of per capita income at a rate designed to attain, at the earliest possible date, levels of income capable of assuring self-sustaining development, and sufficient to make Latin American income levels constantly larger in relation to the levels of the more industrialized nations. In this way the gap between the living standards of Latin America and those of the more developed countries can be narrowed. Similarly, presently existing differences in income levels among the Latin American countries will be reduced by accelerating the development of the relatively less developed countries and granting them maximum priority in the distribution of resources and in international cooperation in general. In evaluating the degree of relative development, account will be taken not only of average levels of real income and gross product per capita, but also of indices of infant mortality, illiteracy, and per capita daily caloric intake.

   It is recognized that, in order to reach these objectives within a reasonable time, the rate of economic growth in any country of Latin America should be not less that 2.5 per cent per capita per year, and that each participating country should determine its own growth target in the light of its stage of social and economic evolution, resource endowment, and ability to mobilize national efforts for development.

2. To make the benefits of economic progress available to all citizens of all economic and social groups through a more equitable distribution of national income, raising more rapidly the income and standard of living of the needier sectors of the population, at the same time that a higher proportion of the national product is devoted to investment.

3. To achieve balanced diversification in national economic structures, both regional and functional, making them increasingly free from dependence on the export of a limited number of primary products and the importation of capital goods while attaining stability in the prices of exports or in income derived from exports.

4. To accelerate the process of rational industrialization so as to increase the productivity of the economy as a whole, taking full advantage of the talents and energies of both the private and public sectors, utilizing the natural resources of the country and providing

productive and remunerative employment for unemployed or part-time workers. Within this process of industrialization, special attention should be given to the establishment and development of capital-goods industries.

5. To raise greatly the level of agricultural productivity and output and to improve related storage, transportation, and marketing services.

6. To encourage, in accordance with the characteristics of each country, programs of comprehensive agrarian reform leading to the effective transformation, where required, of unjust structures and systems of land tenure and use, with a view to replacing latifundia and dwarf holdings by an equitable system of land tenure so that, with the help of timely and adequate credit, technical assistance and facilities for the marketing and distribution of products, the land will become for the man who works it the basis of his economic stability, the foundation of his increasing welfare, and the guarantee of his freedom and dignity.

7. To eliminate adult illiteracy and by 1970 to assure, as a minimum, access to six years of primary education for each school-age child in Latin America; to modernize and expand vocational, secondary and higher educational and training facilities, to strengthen the capacity for basic and applied research; and to provide the competent personnel required in rapidly-growing societies.

8. To increase life expectancy at birth by a minimum of five years, and to increase the ability to learn and produce, by improving individual and public health. To attain this goal it will be necessary, among other measures, to provide adequate potable water supply and sewage disposal to not less than 70 per cent of the urban and 50 per cent of the rural population; to reduce the mortality rate of children less than five years of age by at least one-half; to control the more serious communicable diseases, according to their importance as a cause of sickness, disability, and death; to eradicate those illnesses, especially malaria, for which effective techniques are known; to improve nutrition; to train medical and health personnel to meet at least minimum requirements; to improve basic health services at national and local levels; and to intensify scientific research and apply its results more fully and effectively to the prevention and cure of illness.

9. To increase the construction of low-cost houses for low-income families in order to replace inadequate and deficient housing and to reduce housing shortages; and to provide necessary public services to both urban and rural centers of population.

10. To maintain stable price levels, avoiding inflation or deflation and the consequent social hardships and maldistribution of resources,

always bearing in mind the necessity of maintaining an adequate rate of economic growth.

11. To strengthen existing agreements on economic integration, with a view to the ultimate fulfillment of aspirations for a Latin American common market that will expand and diversify trade among the Latin American countries and thus contribute to the economic growth of the region.

12. To develop cooperative programs designed to prevent the harmful effects of excessive fluctuations in the foreign exchange earnings derived from exports of primary products, which are of vital importance to economic and social development; and to adopt the measures necessary to facilitate the access of Latin American exports to international markets.

TITLE II.   ECONOMIC AND SOCIAL DEVELOPMENT

Chapter I. Basic Requirements for Economic and Social Development

The American republics recognize that to achieve the foregoing goals it will be necessary:

1. That comprehensive and well-conceived national programs of economic and social development, aimed at the achievement of self-sustaining growth, be carried out in accordance with democratic principles.

2. That national programs of economic and social development be based on the principle of self-help—as established in the Act of Bogotá—and on the maximum use of domestic resources, taking into account the special conditions of each country.

3. That in the preparation and execution of plans for economic and social development, women should be placed on an equal footing with men.

4. That the Latin American countries obtain sufficient external financial assistance, a substantial portion of which should be extended on flexible conditions with respect to periods and terms of repayment and forms of utilization, in order to supplement domestic capital formation and reinforce their import capacity; and that, in support of well-conceived programs, which include the necessary structural reforms and measures for the mobilization of internal resources, a supply of capital from all external sources during the coming 10 years of at least 20 billion dollars be made available to the Latin American countries, with priority to the relatively less

developed countries. The greater part of this sum should be in public funds.

5. That institutions in both the public and private sectors, including labor organizations, cooperatives, and commercial, industrial, and financial institutions, be strengthened and improved for the increasing and effective use of domestic resources, and that the social reforms necessary to permit a fair distribution of the fruits of economic and social progress be carried out.

Chapter II. National Development Programs

1. Participating Latin American countries agree to introduce or strengthen systems for the preparation, execution, and periodic revision of national programs for economic and social development consistent with the principles, objectives, and requirements contained in this document. Participating Latin American countries should formulate, if possible within the next eighteen months, long-term development programs. Such programs should embrace, according to the characteristics of each country, the elements outlined in the Appendix.

2. National development programs should incorporate self-help efforts directed to:

   a. Improvement of human resources and widening of opportunities by raising general standards of education and health; improving and extending technical education and professional training with emphasis on science and technology; providing adequate remuneration for work performed, encouraging the talents of managers, entrepreneurs, and wage earners, providing more productive employment for underemployed manpower; establishing effective systems of labor relations, and procedures for consultation and collaboration among public authorities, employer associations, and labor organizations; promoting the establishment and expansion of local institutions for basic and applied research; and improving the standards of public administration.

   b. Wider development and more efficient use of natural resources, especially those which are now idle or under-utilized, including measures for the processing of raw materials.

   c. The strengthening of the agricultural base, progressively extending the benefits of the land to those who work it, and ensuring in countries with Indian populations the integration of these populations into the economic, social, and cultural processes of modern life. To carry out these aims, measures should be adopted, among others, to establish or improve, as the case may be, the following services: extension, credit, technical assistance, agricultural research and mechanization; health and education; storage and distribution; cooperatives and farmer's associations; and community development.

d. More effective, rational and equitable mobilization and use of financial resources through the reform of tax structures, including fair and adequate taxation of large incomes and real estate, and the strict application of measures to improve fiscal administration. Development programs should include the adaptation of budget expenditures to development needs, measures for the maintenance of price stability, the creation of essential credit facilities at reasonable rates of interest, and the encouragement of private savings.

e. Promotion through appropriate measures, including the signing of agreements for the purpose of reducing or eliminating double taxation, of conditions that will encourage the flow of foreign investments and help to increase the capital resources of participating countries in need of capital.

f. Improvement of systems of distribution and sales in order to make markets more competitive and prevent monopolistic practices.

Chapter III. Immediate and Short-Term Action Measures

1. Recognizing that a number of Latin American countries, despite their best efforts, may require emergency financial assistance, the United States will provide assistance from the funds which are or may be established for such purposes. The United States stands ready to take prompt action on applications for such assistance. Applications relating to existing situations should be submitted within the next 60 days.

2. Participating Latin American countries should, in addition to creating or strengthening machinery for long-term development programming, immediately increase their efforts to accelerate their development by giving special emphasis to the following objectives:

a. The completion of projects already under way and the initiation of projects for which the basic studies have been made, in order to accelerate their financing and execution.

b. The implementation of new projects which are designed:

1) To meet the most pressing social needs and benefit directly the greatest number of people;

2) To concentrate efforts within each country in the less developed or more depressed areas in which particularly serious social problems exist;

3) To utilize idle capacity or resources, particularly under-employed manpower; and

4) To survey and assess natural resources.

c. The facilitation of the preparation and execution of long-term programs through measures designed:

1) To train teachers, technicians, and specialists;

2) To provide accelerated training to workers and farmers;

3) To improve basic statistics;

4) To establish needed credit and marketing facilities; and

5) To improve services and administration.

3. The United States will assist in carrying out these short-term measures with a view to achieving concrete results from the Alliance for Progress at the earliest possible moment. In connection with the measures set forth above, and in accordance with the statement of President Kennedy, the United States will provide assistance under the Alliance, including assistance for the financing of short-term measures, totalling more than one billion dollars in the year ending March 1962.

Chapter IV. External Assistance in Support of National Development Programs

1. The economic and social development of Latin America will require a large amount of additional public and private financial assistance on the part of capital-exporting countries, including the members of the Development Assistance Group and international lending agencies. The measures provided for in the Act of Bogotá, and the new measures provided for in this Charter, are designed to create a framework within which such additional assistance can be provided and effectively utilized.

2. The United States will assist those participating countries whose development programs establish self-help measures and economic and social policies and programs consistent with the goals and principles of this Charter. To supplement the domestic efforts of such countries, the United States is prepared to allocate resources which, along with those anticipated from other external sources, will be of a scope and magnitude adequate to realize the goals envisaged in this Charter. Such assistance will be allocated to both social and economic development and, where appropriate, will take the form of grants or loans on flexible terms and conditions. The participating countries will request the assistance of other capital-exporting countries and appropriate institutions so that they may provide assistance for the attainment of these objectives.

3. The United States will assist in the financing of technical assistance projects proposed by a participating country or by the General Secretariat of the Organization of American States for the purpose of:

   a. Providing experts contracted in agreement with governments to work under their direction and to assist them in the preparation of specific investment projects and the strengthening of national mechanisms for preparing projects, using specialized engineering firms where appropriate.

   b. Carrying out, pursuant to existing agreements for cooperation among the General Secretariat of the Organization of American States, the Economic Commission for Latin America, and the Inter-American Development Bank, field investigations and studies, including those relating to development problems, the organization of national planning agencies and the preparation of development programs, agrarian reform and rural development, health, cooperatives, housing, education and professional training, and taxation and tax administration; and

   c. Convening meetings of experts and officials on development and related problems.

   The governments or above mentioned organizations should, when appropriate, seek the cooperation of the United Nations and its specialized agencies in the execution of these activities.

4. The participating Latin American countries recognize that each has in varying degree a capacity to assist fellow republics by providing technical and financial assistance. They recognize that this capacity will increase as their economies grow. They therefore affirm their intention to assist fellow republics increasingly as their individual circumstances permit.

Chapter V. Organization and Procedures

1. In order to provide technical assistance for the formulation of development programs, as may be requested by participating nations, the Organization of American States, the Economic Commission for Latin America, and the Inter-American Development Bank will continue and strengthen their agreements for coordination in this field, in order to have available a group of programming experts whose service can be used to facilitate the implementation of this Charter. The participating countries will also seek an intensification of technical assistance from the specialized agencies of the United Nations for the same purpose.

2. The Inter-American Economic and Social Council, on the joint nomination of the Secretary General of the Organization of

American States, the President of the Inter-American Development Bank, and the Executive Secretary of the United Nations Economic Commission for Latin America, will appoint a panel of nine high-level experts, exclusively on the basis of their experience, technical ability, and competence in the various aspects of economic and social development. The experts may be of any nationality, though if of Latin American origin an appropriate geographical distribution will be sought. They will be attached to the Inter-American Economic and Social Council, but will nevertheless enjoy complete autonomy in the performance of their duties. They may not hold any other remunerative position. The appointment of these experts will be for a period of three years, and may be renewed.

3. Each government, if it so wishes, may present its program for economic and social development for consideration by an ad hoc committee, composed of no more than three members drawn from the panel of experts referred to in the preceding paragraph together with an equal number of experts not on the panel. The experts who compose the ad hoc committee will be appointed by the Secretary General of the Organization of American States at the request of the interested government and with its consent.

4. The committee will study the development program, exchange opinions with the interested government as to possible modifications and, with the consent of the government, report its conclusions to the Inter-American Development Bank and to other governments and institutions that may be prepared to extend external financial and technical assistance in connection with the execution of the program.

5. In considering a development program presented to it, the ad hoc committee will examine the consistency of the program with the principles of the Act of Bogotá and of this Charter, taking into account the elements in the Appendix.

6. The General Secretariat of the Organization of American States will provide the personnel needed by the experts referred to in paragraphs 2 and 3 of this Chapter in order to fulfill their tasks. Such personnel may be employed specifically for this purpose or may be made available from the permanent staffs of the Organization of American States, the Economic Commission for Latin America, and the Inter-American Development Bank, in accordance with the present liaison arrangements between the three organizations. The General Secretariat of the Organization of American States may seek arrangements with the United Nations Secretariat, its specialized agencies and the Inter-American Specialized Organizations, for the temporary assignment of necessary personnel.

7. A government whose development program has been the object of recommendations made by the ad hoc committee with respect to

external financing requirements may submit the program to the Inter-American Development Bank so that the Bank may undertake the negotiations required to obtain such financing, including the organization of a consortium of credit institutions and governments disposed to contribute to the continuing and systematic financing, on appropriate terms, of the development program. However, the government will have full freedom to resort through any other channels to all sources of financing, for the purpose of obtaining, in full or in part, the required resources.

The ad hoc committee shall not interfere with the right of each government to formulate its own goals, priorities, and reforms in its national development programs.

The recommendations of the ad hoc committee will be of great importance in determining the distribution of public funds under the Alliance for Progress which contribute to the external financing of such programs. These recommendations shall give special consideration to Title I. 1.

The participating governments will also use their good offices to the end that these recommendations may be accepted as a factor of great importance in the decisions taken, for the same purpose, by inter-American credit institutions, other international credit agencies, and other friendly governments which may be potential sources of capital.

8. The Inter-American Economic and Social Council will review annually the progress achieved in the formulation, national implementation, and international financing of development programs; and will submit to the Council of the Organization of American States such recommendations as it deems pertinent.

Appendix: Elements of National Development Programs

1. The establishment of mutually consistent targets to be aimed at over the program period in expanding productive capacity in industry, agriculture, mining, transport, power and communications, and in improving conditions of urban and rural life, including better housing, education and health.

2. The assignment of priorities and the description of methods to achieve the targets, including specific measures and major projects. Specific development projects should be justified in terms of their relative costs and benefits, including their contribution to social productivity.

3. The measures which will be adopted to direct the operations of the public sector and to encourage private action in support of the development program.

4. The estimated cost, in national and foreign currency, of major projects and of the development program as a whole, year by year over the program period.

5. The internal resources, public and private, estimated to become available for the execution of the programs.

6. The direct and indirect effects of the program on the balance of payments, and the external financing, public and private, estimated to be required for the execution of the program.

7. The basic fiscal and monetary policies to be followed in order to permit implementation of the program within a framework of price stability.

8. The machinery of public administration—including relationships with local governments, decentralized agencies and nongovernmental organizations, such as labor organizations, cooperatives, business and industrial organizations—to be used in carrying out the program, adapting it to changing circumstances and evaluating the progress made.

TITLE III.   ECONOMIC INTEGRATION OF LATIN AMERICA

The American Republics consider that the broadening of present national markets in Latin America is essential to accelerate the process of economic development in the Hemisphere. It is also an appropriate means for obtaining greater productivity through specialized and complementary industrial production which will, in turn, facilitate the attainment of greater social benefits for the inhabitants of the various regions of Latin America. The broadening of markets will also make possible the better use of resources under the Alliance for Progress. Consequently, the American republics recognize that:

1. The Montevideo Treaty (because of its flexibility and because it is open to adherence of all of the Latin American nations) and the Central American Treaty on Economic Integration are appropriate instruments for the attainment of these objectives, as was recognized in Resolution No. 11 (III) of the Ninth Session of the Economic Commission for Latin America.

2. The integration process can be intensified and accelerated not only by the specialization resulting from the broadening of markets through the liberalization of trade but also through the use of such instruments as the agreements for complementary production within economic sectors provided for in the Montevideo Treaty.

3. In order to insure the balanced and complementary economic expansion of all of the countries involved, the integration process should take into account, on a flexible basis, the condition of countries at a relatively less advanced stage of economic development, permitting them to be granted special, fair, and equitable treatment.

4. In order to facilitate economic integration in Latin America, it is advisable to establish effective relationships between the Latin American Free Trade Association and the group of countries adhering to the Central American Economic Integration Treaty, as well as between either of these groups and other Latin American countries. These arrangements should be established within the limits determined by these instruments.

5. The Latin American countries should coordinate their actions to meet the unfavorable treatment accorded to their foreign trade in world markets, particularly that resulting from certain restrictive and discriminatory policies of extracontinental countries and economic groups.

6. In the application of resources under the Alliance for Progress, special attention should be given not only to investments for multinational projects that will contribute to strengthening the integration process in all its aspects, but also to the necessary financing of industrial production, and to the growing expansion of trade in industrial products within Latin America.

7. In order to facilitate the participation of countries at a relatively lower stage of economic development in multinational Latin American economic cooperation programs, and in order to promote the balanced and harmonious development of the Latin American integration process, special attention should be given to the needs of these countries in the administration of financial resources provided under the Alliance for Progress, particularly in connection with infrastructure programs and the promotion of new lines of production.

8. The economic integration process implies a need for additional investment in various fields of economic activity and funds provided under the Alliance for Progress should cover these needs as well as those required for the financing of national development programs.

9. When groups of Latin American countries have their own institutions for financing economic integration, the financing referred to in the preceding paragraph should preferably be channeled through these institutions. With respect to regional financing designed to further the purposes of existing regional integration instruments, the

cooperation of the Inter-American Development Bank should be sought in channeling extra-regional contributions which may be granted for these purposes.

10. One of the possible means for making effective a policy for the financing of Latin American integration would be to approach the International Monetary Fund and other financial sources with a view to providing a means for solving temporary balance-of-payments problems that may occur in countries participating in economic integration arrangements.

11. The promotion and coordination of transportation and communications systems is an effective way to accelerate the integration process. In order to counteract abusive practices in relation to freight rates and tariffs, it is advisable to encourage the establishment of multinational transport and communication enterprises in the Latin American countries, or to find other appropriate solutions.

12. In working toward economic integration and complementary economies, efforts should be made to achieve an appropriate coordination of national plans, or to engage in joint planning for various economies through the existing regional integration organizations. Efforts should also be made to promote an investment policy directed to the progressive elimination of unequal growth rates in the different geographic areas, particularly in the case of countries which are relatively less developed.

13. It is necessary to promote the development of national Latin American enterprises, in order that they may compete on an equal footing with foreign enterprises.

14. The active participation of the private sector is essential to economic integration and development, and except in those countries in which free enterprise does not exist, development planning by the pertinent national public agencies, far from hindering such participation, can facilitate and guide it, thus opening new perspectives for the benefit of the community.

15. As the countries of the Hemisphere still under colonial domination achieve their independence, they should be invited to participatin in Latin American economic integration programs.

TITLE IV.   BASIC EXPORT COMMODITIES

The American Republics recognize that the economic development of Latin America requires expansion of its trade, a simultaneous and corresponding increase in foreign exchange incomes received from exports, a lessening of cyclical or seasonal fluctuations in the incomes of those countries that still depend heavily on the export of raw materials, and the correction of the secular deterioration in their terms of trade.

They therefore agree that the following measures should be taken:

Chapter I. National Measures

National measures affecting commerce in primary products should be directed and applied to in order to:

1. Avoid undue obstacles to the expansion of trade in these products;
2. Avoid market instability;
3. Improve the efficiency of international plans and mechanisms for stabilization; and
4. Increase their present markets and expand their area of trade at a rate compatible with rapid development.

Therefore:

A. Importing member countries should reduce and if possible eliminate, as soon as feasible, all restrictions and discriminatory practices affecting the consumption and importation of primary products, including those with the highest possible degree of processing in the country of origin, except when these restrictions are imposed temporarily for purposes of economic diversification, to hasten the economic development of less developed nations, or to establish basic national reserves. Importing countries should also be ready to support, by adequate regulations, stabilization programs for primary products that may be agreed upon with producing countries.

B. Industrialized countries should give special attention to the need for hastening economic development of less developed countries. Therefore, they should make maximum efforts to create conditions, compatible with their international obligations, through which they may extend advantages to less developed countries so as to permit the rapid expansion of their markets. In view of the great need for this rapid development, industrialized countries should also study ways in which to modify, wherever possible, international commitments which prevent the achievement of this objective.

C. Producing member countries should formulate their plans for production and export, taking account of their effect on world markets and of the necessity of supporting and improving the effectiveness of international stablization programs and mechanisms. Similarly they should try to avoid increasing the uneconomic production of goods which can be obtained under better conditions in the less developed countries of the Continent, in which the production of these goods is an important source of employment.

D. Member countries should adopt all necessary measures to direct technological studies toward finding new uses and by-products of those primary commodities that are most important to their economies.

E. Member countries should try to reduce, and, if possible, eliminate within a reasonable time export subsidies and other measures which cause instability in the markets for basic commodities and excessive fluctuations in prices and income.

Chapter II. International Cooperation Measures

1. Member countries should make coordinated, and if possible, joint efforts designed:

   a. To eliminate as soon as possible undue protection of the production of basic products;

   b. To eliminate taxes and reduce excessive domestic prices which discourage the consumption of imported basic products;

   c. To seek to end preferential agreements and other measures which limit world consumption of Latin American basic products and their access to international markets, especially the markets of Western European countries in process of economic integration, and of countries with centrally planned economies; and

   d. To adopt the necessary consultation mechanisms so that their marketing policies will not have damaging effects on the stability of the markets for basic commodities.

2. Industrialized countries should give maximum cooperation to less developed countries so that their raw material exports will have the greatest degree of processing that is economic.

3. Through their representation in international financial organizations, member countries should suggest that these organizations, when considering loans for the promotion of production for export, take into account the effect of such loans on products which are in surplus in world markets.

4. Member countries should support the efforts being made by international commodity study groups and by the Commission on International Commodity Trade of the United Nations. In this connection, it should be considered that producing and consuming nations bear a joint responsibility for taking national and international steps to reduce market instability.

5. The Secretary General of the Organization of American States shall convene a group of experts appointed by their respective Governments to meet before Novemeber 30, 1961 and to report, not later

than March 31, 1962 on measures to provide an adequate and
effective means of offsetting the effects of fluctuations in the
volume and prices of exports of basic products. The experts shall:

   a. Consider the questions regarding compensatory financing raised
     during the present meeting;

   b. Analyze the proposal for establishing an international fund for
     the stabilization of export receipts contained in the Report of the
     Group of Experts to the Special Meeting of the Inter-American
     Economic and Social Council, as well as any other alternative
     proposals;

   c. Prepare a draft plan for the creation of mechanisms for
     compensatory financing. This draft plan should be circulated
     among the member Governments and their opinions obtained
     well in advance of the next meeting of the Commission on
     International Commodity Trade.

6. Member countries should support the efforts under way to improve
   and strengthen international commodity agreements and should be
   prepared to cooperate in the solution of specific commodity
   problems. Furthermore, they should endeavor to adopt adequate
   solutions for the short- and long-term problems affecting markets for
   such commodities so that the economic interests of producers and
   consumers are equally safeguarded.

7. Member countries should request other producer and consumer
   countries to cooperate in stabilization programs, bearing in mind
   that the raw materials of the Western Hemisphere are also produced
   and consumed in other parts of the world.

8. Member countries recognize that the disposal of accumulated
   reserves and surpluses can be a means of achieving the goals outlined
   in the first chapter of this Title, provided that, along with the
   generation of local resources, the consumption of essential products
   in the receiving countries is immediately increased. The disposal of
   surpluses and reserves should be carried out in an orderly manner, in
   order to:

   a. Avoid disturbing existing commercial markets in member coun-
     tries, and

   b. Encourage expansion of the sale of their products to other
     markets.

However, it is recognized that:

   a. The disposal of surpluses should not displace commercial sales of
     identical products traditionally carried out by other countries;
     and

    b. Such disposal cannot substitute for large scale financial and technical assistance programs.

In witness whereof this Charter is signed, in Punta del Este, Uruguay, on the seventeenth day of August, nineteen hundred sixty-one.

The original texts shall be deposited in the archives of the Pan American Union, through the Secretary General of the Special Meeting, in order that certified copies may be sent to the Governments of the Member States of the Organization of American States.

Thomas C. Mann

The Democratic Ideal in Our Policy
Toward Latin America[1]

Thirty years ago this month I received a law degree and started out as a young lawyer. Then we were in the throes of the Great Depression and preoccupied with our domestic economic problems. Students on campus were not greatly concerned about foreign affairs in those days.

Today the members of the graduating class of this great Christian university will start their careers at a time when our nation marches forward to new horizons of economic opportunity, individual dignity and social justice. Technological advances have, however, presented us with new challenges and new opportunities in our relations with other countries. We are caught up, as it were, in a shrinking, interdependent world in which we have great responsibilities and which has suddenly become complex. We can no longer afford to live apart from the rest of the world as if it did not vitally affect our national and individual well-being.

The problems which faced my graduating class thirty years ago, formidable as they seemed to us at the time, were certainly much more elementary, much more simple, and by comparison much less important, than those which face what Latin Americans would call your "Generation of 1964."

Within this framework, I would like briefly to discuss with you today one of the problems of our Latin American foreign policy—the problem of what it is we can do to bring about a more effective exercise of representative democracy in the Western Hemisphere. There is no subject concerning our Latin American foreign policy which has over the years generated more debate or a debate which has generated so much heat and, it seems at times, so little light.

[1]Commencement Address at the University of Notre Dame, June 7, 1964.

I

The first point I wish to make is that United States foreign policy is firmly and irrevocably committed to the principle that every individual, no matter in what part of the world he lives, has an inalienable right to his individual freedom and to his individual dignity.

For his day, as well as for ours, Benjamin Franklin spoke for the nation when he expressed the hope that

> a thorough knowledge of the Rights of Man may pervade all nations of the earth, so that a philosopher may set his foot anywhere on its surface and say 'This is my country.'

More recently, President Johnson, in speaking of the Charter of the Alliance for Progress, expressed somewhat the same thought in different words:

> Our Charter charges each American country to seek and to strengthen representative democracy. Without that democracy and without the freedom that it nourishes, material progress is an aimless enterprise, destroying the dignity of the spirit that it is really meant to liberate. So we will continue to join with you and encourage democracy until we build a Hemisphere of free nations from the Tierra del Fuego to the Arctic Circle.

II

The example of a vigorous representative democracy in the United States that assures equality and dignity to all of our citizens will provide strong support for our policy. A policy of consistent persuasion in discussions with our Latin American friends is another way to help promote democratic progress in the hemisphere.

It has long been, and continues to be, our firm policy to discourage any who conspire to overthrow constitutionally elected governments. But if governments are overthrown, it has long been our practice, in ways compatible with the sovereignty and the national dignity of others, to encourage the holding of free and fair elections—to encourage a return to constitutional procedures. Other American Republics make equally valuable contributions to building a western hemisphere tradition of democracy by their example, by the strength of their moral positions, and by expressions of their principles.

It is understandable that all of us sometimes become impatient with the rate of progress towards making this ideal a reality everywhere. We have not yet reached perfection in our own country. Many American Republics have made great progress in establishing a democratic tradition within the last few decades. In others, democracy seems at times to take two steps forward only to be temporarily pushed back a step. In Cuba, the light of democracy has temporarily been extinguished.

But we should not, I think, judge either the rate or degree of hemisphere progress towards democracy solely by the number of *coups d'etat* which take place. The degree of individual freedom which exists in the hemisphere, the average life span of *de facto* governments, the extent of political repression, the degree of freedom of the press and of peaceful assembly, and the growing number of people in the hemisphere who consistently support the principle of free and periodic elections, are also relevant yardsticks.

If one looks at the forest instead of the trees, he can see that these quiet, unpublicized efforts on the part of the United States and other American Republics have, along with many other factors, contributed to a wider and deeper observance of the forms of representative democracy in this hemisphere and, perhaps even more important, to a growing respect by governments, in deeds as well as words, for the dignity of man and for his basic human rights. I am confident that the general movement will continue to be forward; I hope it can be accelerated.

III

One way to bring about more rapid progress is by collective action of the community of American States.

As early as 1837, Pedro Vicuña of Chile urged the establishment of a General Congress of American States to oppose tyranny.

In 1945 the Uruguayan Government proposed the doctrine that there is a "parallelism" between peace and democracy. The United States supported this thesis. Only eight American Republics including the United States voted affirmatively for the Uruguayan proposal.

In 1960, at a meeting of Foreign Ministers in San José, the United States again supported collective action and introduced a new concept: Support of the ideal of representative democracy should not merely be negative in the sense of opposition to a particular dictatorial regime; it should positively ensure, by collective action, that peoples have an opportunity, in free and fair elections, to express their will—so that a Batista will not again be followed by a Castro. There was little support for this thesis at the time although the majority, including the United States, did vote for sanctions against the Trujillo regime.

More recently, Venezuela has taken the lead in proposing informally that the American States agree to consult together when unconstitutional changes of government occur in the hemisphere. We have long since assured the Venezuelan Government of our support.

I would hope that the Venezuelan initiative will be but a step in a future process of developing a new international procedure which, while safeguarding the essential sovereign rights of every nation, defines with care and precision the kinds of violations of basic human rights which are, to use the phrases of a former Secretary of State, of such a "flagrant and notorious character" that they have a "relationship to the maintenance of international peace and security" and hence justify such collective action as may be agreed upon. If this were done, tyranny of the kind we saw under Trujillo and which we still see under Castro today, could be effectively and legally dealt with.

IV

It is sometimes said that since the American community of nations has failed to take effective collective action to eliminate dictatorships in the hemisphere, the United States—unilaterally and alone—should undertake to force all Latin American governments to stay on the path of constitutionality. The United States has had a rather full experience in attempting, with the best of motives, to impose democracy on other countries. It is worthwhile to recall them.

Monroe's Declaration of 1823, in its original intent, was a shield for Latin America against European powers seeking to recover lost colonies and to expand their territories. In the three instances in which it was applied in the manner originally intended—in 1864, 1895 and 1902—it was of considerable help to the Latin American states directly involved.

But in 1904 Theodore Roosevelt presented his now famous corollary:

Chronic wrongdoing—may in America—ultimately require intervention by some civilized nation—in the exercise of an international police power.

The philosophy underlying the Roosevelt corollary was not new; the Platt amendment which impaired Cuban sovereignty was already an accomplished fact. But it did open the way for a number of new adventures. In 1906 and 1909 the Marines were sent to Cuba, in 1909 and 1912 to Nicaragua, in 1912 to the Dominican Republic, in 1915 to Haiti.

In 1913, a new moral dimension was added to the Roosevelt corollary in an attempt to justify additional United States interventions. It was stated in these words:

Cooperation is possible only when supported at every turn by the orderly processes of just government based upon law, not upon arbitrary or irregular force . . . .

Under this doctrine we engaged in a new series of interventions in Mexico. These led to the occupation of Veracruz and to Pershing's expedition. They brought us to the verge of war with our southern neighbor at the very time we were being drawn into the First World War.

Arthur Whitaker in his book *The Western Hemisphere Idea,* comes to this conclusion:

Protective imperialism (under the 1904 corollary) would intervene to correct situations of chronic wrongdoing and chaos only to the extent necessary to prevent European intervention and then withdraw. The civilizing mission (the 1913 policy), on the other hand, had no such *ad hoc* character or limited objective. The missionary's work is not done when the devils have been cast out; it has hardly begun. He must stay on until he has taught his charges how to lead the good life, and that may take quite a long time. (Parenthetical matter added.)

And Howard Cline, in speaking of the 1913 doctrine, reminds us in his book, *The United States and Mexico:*

Thus there were 'good' revolutions and 'bad' revolutions . . . The latter brought only venal, unidealistic people to power, while the former put the particular nation back on the constitutional track . . . . As events in Mexico and elsewhere ultimately showed, the test of 'constitutional legitimacy' was unworkable, especially in Latin America. The United States . . . renounced it as a national policy in 1921 . . . .

The words of these two distinguished scholars may, from our point of view, seem rather harsh. Certainly our intentions were good. But few knowledgeable people will deny that they accurately reflect Latin America's bitter reaction to our interventionist activities under doctrines of 1904 and 1913.

Our interventions were, in the Latin American point of view, patronizing in the extreme. By making the United States the sole judge of Latin America's political morality, they were degrading to proud peoples who believed that, in their own wars of independence, they had earned the right to manage their own affairs—to be masters in their own houses. They produced schismatic tendencies in the inter-American family and brought our relations with Latin America to an all-time low.

These historical experiences suggest two things: Unilateral United States interventions in the hemisphere have never succeeded, in themselves, in restoring constitutional government for any appreciable period of time. And they have, in every case, left for our country a legacy of suspicion and resentment which has endured long after our interventions were abandoned as impracticable.

As Cline has observed:

The lengthy record of discord during the years 1913 and 1914 carries its own lessons. One is that international problems are more complex than slogan-makers sometimes assume. A worthy set of attitudes is no substitute for coherent policy.

Franklin Roosevelt surely had these lessons of history in mind when he not only pledged the United States to the policy of non-intervention but defined his policy of the "Good Neighbor" as:

... the neighbor who resolutely respects himself, and, because he does so, respects the rights of others—the neighbor who respects his obligations and respects the sanctity of his agreements in and with a world of neighbors.

Two wrongs do not make a right. We cannot achieve a peaceful world ruled by law if we do not live up to our own obligations.

As an answer to the United States interventionist doctrines, Latin Americans developed doctrines of their own. Let there be no mistake: these Latin American counter-doctrines were "tailor-made" for the United States; their purpose was to bring an end to United States interventions. I shall mention only one:

By 1928, when the Sixth International Conference of American States met at Habana, a proposal was introduced which stated the simple proposition that "No state has the right to interfere in the internal affairs of another."

After a long and somewhat acrimonious debate the United States managed to prevent adoption of the resolution, but the handwriting was on the wall. In 1933, at the Seventh Conference in Montevideo, the United States accepted the doctrine of non-intervention with qualifications. In 1936, at Buenos Aires, we accepted it unconditionally.

This Latin American doctrine of non-intervention is now written into the Charter of the Organization of American States. It is a treaty of obligation. Allow me to read to you Articles 15 and 16 of the Charter:

Article 15. No State or group of States has the right to intervene, directly or indirectly, for any reason whatever, in the internal or external affairs of any other State. The foregoing prohibits not only armed force but also any other form of interference or attempted threat against the personality of the State or against its political, economic or cultural elements.

Article 16. No State may use or encourage the use of coercive measures of an economic or political character in order to force the sovereign will of another State and obtain from it advantages of any kind.

As the scholars Thomas point out in their study of *Non-Intervention:*

The essence of intervention is the attempt to compel.

All of this does not mean that we will in the future recognize all governments which come into power in an unconstitutional manner. Each case must be looked at in the light of its own facts. Where the facts warrant it—where the circumstances are such, to use someone else's phrase, as to "outrage the conscience of America"—we reserve our freedom to register our indignation by refusing to recognize or to continue our economic cooperation.

It does mean that, consistent with our treaty obligations, we cannot put ourselves in a doctrinaire straightjacket (sic) of automatic application of sanctions to every unconstitutional regime in the hemisphere with the obvious intention of dictating internal political developments in other countries. As the facts amply demonstrate, this is no departure from the practice which has prevailed in the most recent years.

The third point to which I invite your attention is this: Unilateral intervention for the purpose of forcing constitutional changes in another country does not always serve either the cause of democracy or the national security interests of the United States.

To illustrate, not long ago a majority of the Guatemalan people voted in free elections for Arbenz, a candidate for president. Later the Guatemalan people discovered that Arbenz was a Marxist-Leninist. Colonel Castillo led a successful revolt and was widely acclaimed by his people when he marched into Guatemala City. Had we been unconditionally committed to the support of all constitutional governments under all circumstances, we would have been obliged to do everything within our power to bring about the overthrow of Castillo and to restore a Marxist-Leninist to power against the will of the Guatemalan people.

The question of our relationships with Communist regimes in this hemisphere is, of course, a separate subject and is beyond the scope of these remarks. It raises separate questions, such as our inherent right of self-defense and measures, under existing treaties, to deal with situations which threaten the peace and security of the hemisphere.

V

Against this background, what conclusions are to be drawn? What can we do to help make the democratic ideal a reality in this hemisphere? I offer the following suggestions:

First, we should continue, in our bilateral discussions with other governments, to encourage democracy in the quiet, unpublicized way and on the day-to-day basis that I have already referred to; and we should support parallel efforts of other American states. If there is no intent to force the will of a sovereign government this tactic is entirely compatible with our commitments and with the dignity and self-respect of others.

Second, we should support appropriate measures for broadening the scope of collective action with the aim of addressing ourselves first to those cases where repression, tyranny and brutality outrage the conscience of mankind. I can think of no way in which the American community of states can better serve the cause of human dignity, individual and national freedom and representative democracy than to develop a set of procedures for dealing with this type of problem. The

United States has never believed that collective action for such purposes is proscribed by the Charter of the Organization of American States; but if the majority of the member States are of a contrary opinion, then let us amend the Charter.

Third, in each case where a government is over-thrown by force there should be a careful, dispassionate assessment of each situation in the light of all the surrounding facts and circumstances so that decisions concerning recognition, trade, aid and other related matters can be made which are consistent with our ideals, with international law, and with our over-all national interests.

In making this assessment, regard should also be paid to the fact that not only is each American Republic different from all the others but that each *de facto* government is likewise different in its aims, its motives, its policies, and in the kinds of problems it faces.

Fourth, if as a result of this appraisal, a decision is made not to recognize a regime—and this may well be the case in the future as it has been in the past—then it should be made clear that non-recognition is based squarely on a failure on the part of another government to abide by the established rules of international conduct.

Fifth, when the decision is made to recognize a regime, it should be clear that there is no basis under international law for equating recognition with United States approval of the internal political policies and practices of another government. Resolution 35 of the Ninth Inter-American Conference of American States makes this point very clear. It declares:

That the establishment or maintenance of diplomatic relations with a government does not imply any judgment upon the domestic policy of that government.

Sixth, we should continue our established practice of consulting with other American Republics whenever a question of recognition arises.

Finally, let there be no mistake about our consistent and complete devotion to the principles of human dignity and freedom of the individual. We believe that these principles can only be realized in a democratic political system in which governments are the servants of the people and responsive to their will. They are a central element in our foreign policy towards Latin America. We shall in every way consistent with our obligations continue our efforts to help make democracy a reality throughout the entire hemisphere.

●   ●   ●

As is often the case, there is more to be said than time allows for. I have already presumed on your courtesy by speaking so long. But if I am permitted one word of counsel, it would be this:

I hope you will feel a pride in your university, your church, and your country and in the efforts they are all making to create a peaceful world, ruled by law and Christian charity which is devoted to both the material and spiritual progress of all mankind in freedom. And I hope that you will look to the future with confidence that freedom and not tyranny is the "wave of the future" in this hemisphere. I think you will see even greater progress towards freedom in your generation than the impressive gains I have seen in my time.

Richard M. Nixon

Action for Progress for the Americas[1]

Mr. Chairman, ladies and gentlemen of the Inter-American Press Association, I welcome this opportunity to speak to you and to our neighbors throughout the new world about a matter uppermost in the minds and hearts of all of us. I want to speak to you about the state of our partnership in the Americas. In doing so, I wish to place before you some suggestions for reshaping and re-invigorating that partnership.

Often we in the United States have been charged with an overweening confidence in the rightness of our own prescriptions: occasionally we have been guilty of the charge. I intend to correct that. Therefore, my words tonight are meant as an invitation by one partner for further interchange, for increased communication, and above all for new imagination in meeting our shared responsibilities.

For years, we in the United States have pursued the illusion that we could re-make continents. Conscious of our wealth and technology, seized by the force of our good intentions, driven by our habitual impatience, remembering the dramatic success of the Marshall Plan in postwar Europe, we have sometimes imagined that we knew what was best for everyone else and that we could and should make it happen.

But experience has taught us better.

It has taught us that economic and social development is not an achievement of one nation's foreign policy, but something deeply rooted in each nation's own traditions.

It has taught us that aid that infringes pride is no favor.

It has taught us that each nation, and each region, must be true to its own character.

What I hope we can achieve, therefore, is a more mature partnership in which all voices are heard and none is predominant—a partnership guided by a

[1]Address to the Inter-American Press Association, October 31, 1969.

healthy awareness that give-and-take is better than take-it-or-leave-it.

My suggestions this evening for new directions toward a more balanced relationship come from many sources.

First, they are rooted in my personal convictions. I have seen the problems of the Hemisphere at first hand, and I have felt its surging spirit—determined to break the grip of outmoded structures, yet equally determined to avoid social disintegration. Freedom—justice—a chance for each of our people to live a better and more abundant life—these are goals to which I am unshakably committed. Progress in our Hemisphere is not only a practical necessity but a moral imperative.

Second, these new approaches have been substantially shaped by the report of Governor Rockefeller, who, at my request, listened perceptively to the voices of our neighbors and incorporated their thoughts into a set of foresighted proposals.

Third, they are consistent with thoughts expressed in the Consensus of Viña del Mar, which we have studied with great care.

Fourth, they have benefited from the counsel of many persons in government and out, in this country and throughout the Hemisphere.

And, finally, basically, they reflect the concern of the people of the United States for the development and progress of a Hemisphere which is new in spirit, and which—through our efforts together—we can make new in accomplishment.

I offer no grandiose promises and no panaceas.

I do offer action.

The actions I propose represent a new approach, based on five principles:

First, a firm commitment to the inter-American system, and to the compacts which bind us in that system—as exemplified by the Organization of American States and by the priniciples so nobly set forth in its charter.

Second, respect for national identity and national dignity, in a partnership in which rights and responsibilities are shared by a community of independent states.

Third, a firm commitment to continued U.S. assistance for Hemisphere development.

Fourth, a belief that the principal future pattern of this assistance must be U.S. support for Latin American initiatives, and that this can best be achieved on a multilateral basis within the inter-American system.

Fifth, a dedication to improving the quality of life in the Western Hemisphere—to making people the center of our concerns, and to helping meet their economic, social and human needs.

We have heard many voices from Latin America in these first months of our new Administration—voices of hope, voices of concern, voices of frustration.

We have listened.

Those voices have told us they wanted fewer promises and more action. They have told us that U.S. aid programs seemed to have helped the United States more than Latin America. They have told us our trade policies were insensitive to Latin American needs. They have told us that if our partnership is to thrive, or even to survive, we must recognize that the nations of Latin America must go forward in their own way, under their own leadership.

It is not my purpose here tonight to discuss the extent to which we consider the various charges right or wrong. But I recognize the concerns, and I share many of them. What I propose tonight is, I believe, responsive to those concerns.

The most pressing concerns center on economic development—and especially on the policies by which aid is administered and by which trade is regulated.

In proposing specific changes tonight, I mean these as examples of the actions I believe are possible in a new kind of partnership.

Our partnership should be one in which the United States lectures less and listens more, and in which clear, consistent procedures are established to ensure that the shaping of Latin America's future reflects the will of the Latin American nations.

I believe this requires a number of changes.

To begin with, it requires a fundamental change in the way in which we manage development assistance in the Hemisphere.

I propose that a multilateral inter-American agency be given an increasing share of responsibility for development assistance decisions. CIAP—the Inter-American Committee for the Alliance for Progress—could be given this function. Or an entirely new agency could be created. Whatever the form, the objective would be to evolve an effective multilateral framework for bilateral assistance, to provide the agency with an expert international staff and, over time, to give it major operational and decision-making responsibilities.

The Latin American nations themselves would thus jointly assume a primary role in setting priorities within the Hemisphere, in developing realistic programs, and in keeping their own performance under critical review.

One of the areas most urgently in need of new policies is trade. In order to finance their import needs and to achieve self-sustaining growth, the Latin American nations must expend (sic) their exports.

Most Latin American exports now are raw materials and foodstuffs. We are attempting to help the other countries of the Hemisphere to stabilize their earnings from those exports, and to increase them as time goes on.

Increasingly, however, those countries will have to turn toward manufactured and semi-manufactured products for balanced development and major export growth. Thus they need to be assured of access to the expanding markets of the industrialized world. In order to help achieve this, I have determined to take the following major steps:

> First, to lead a vigorous effort to reduce the non-tariff barriers to trade maintained by nearly all industrialized countries against products of particular interest to Latin American and other developing countries.

> Second, to support increased technical and financial assistance to promote Latin American trade expansion.

> Third, to support the establishment, within the inter-American system, of regular procedures for advance consultation on all trade matters. U.S. trade policies often have a heavy impact on our neighbors. It seems only fair that in the more balanced relationship we seek, there should be full consultation within the Hemisphere family before decisions affecting its members are taken, not after.

> Finally, in world trade forums to press for a liberal system of generalized tariff preferences for all developing countries, including Latin America. We will seek adoption by all of the industrialized countries of a scheme with broad product coverage and with no ceilings on preferential imports. We will seek equal access to industrial markets for all developing countries so as to eliminate the discrimination against Latin America that now exists in many countries. We will also urge that such a system eliminates the inequitable "reverse preferences" that now discriminate against Western Hemisphere countries.

There are three other important economic issues that directly involve the new partnership concept, and which a number of our partners have raised: "tied" loans, debt service and regional economic integration.

For several years now, virtually all loans made under U.S. aid programs have been "tied"—that is, they have been encumbered with restrictions designed to maintain U.S. exports, including a requirement that the money be spent on purchases in the United States. These restrictions have been burdensome for the borrowers, and have impaired the effectiveness of the aid. In June, I ordered the most cumbersome restrictions removed. In addition, I am now ordering that effective November 1, loan dollars sent to Latin America under AID be freed to allow purchases not only here, but anywhere in Latin America. As a third step, I am also ordering that all other onerous conditions and restrictions on U.S. assistance loans be reviewed, with the objective of modifying or eliminating them.

If I might add a personal word, this decision on freeing AID loans is one of those things that people kept saying ought to be done but could not be done. In light of our own balance of payments problems, there were compelling arguments against it. But I felt the needs of the Hemisphere had to come first, so I simply ordered it done—showing our commitment in actions, rather than only in words. This will be our guiding principle in the future.

The growing burden of external debt service has increasingly become a major problem of future development. Some countries find themselves making heavy payments in debt service which reduce the positive effects of development aid. I suggest that CIAP might appropriately urge the international financial organizations to recommend possible remedies.

We have seen a number of moves in Latin America toward regional economic integration, such as the establishment of the Central American Common Market, the Latin American and Caribbean Free Trade Areas, and the Andean Group. The decisions on how far and how fast this process of integration goes, of course, are not ours to make. But I do want to stress that we stand ready to help in this effort, if our help should be wanted.

On all these matters, we look forward to consulting further with our Hemisphere partners. In a major, related move, I am also directing our representatives to invite CIAP, as a regular procedure, to conduct a periodic review of U.S. economic policies as they affect the other nations of the Hemisphere, and to consult with us about them. Similar reviews are now made of the other Hemisphere countries' policies, but the United States has not previously opened its policies to such consultation. I believe true partnership requires that we should, and henceforth, if our partners so desire, we shall.

I would like to turn now to a vital subject in connection with economic development in the Hemisphere, namely, the role of private investment. Clearly, each government must make its own decisions about the place of private investment, domestic and foreign, in its development process. Each must decide for itself whether it wishes to accept or forego the benefits private investment can bring.

For a developing country, constructive foreign investment has the special advantage of being a prime vehicle for the transfer of technology. And certainly, from no other source is so much investment capital available. As we all have seen, however, just as a capital-exporting nation cannot expect another country to accept investors against its will, so must a capital-importing country expect a serious impairment of its ability to attract investment funds when it acts against existing investments in a way which runs counter to commonly accepted norms of international law and behavior. And unfortunately, and perhaps unfairly, such acts by one nation affect investor confidence in the entire region.

We will not encourage U.S. private investment where it is not wanted, or where local political conditions face it with unwarranted risks. But my own strong belief is that properly motivated private enterprise has a vital role to play in social as well as economic development. We have seen it work in our own country. We have seen it work in other countries, whether they are developing or developed, that lately have been recording the world's most spectacular rates of economic growth.

In line with this belief, we are examining ways to modify our direct investment controls in order to help meet the investment requirements of developing nations in Latin America and elsewhere. I have further directed that our aid programs place increasing emphasis on assistance to locally-owned private enterprise. I am also directing that we expand our technical assistance for establishing national and regional capital markets.

As we all have seen, in this age of rapidly advancing science, the challenge of development is only partly economic. Science and technology increasingly hold the key to our national futures. If the promise of this final third of the Twentieth Century is to be realized, the wonders of science must be turned to the service of man.

In the Consensus of Viña del Mar, we were asked for an unprecedented effort to share our scientific and technological capabilities.

To that request, we shall respond in a spirit of partnership.

This, I pledge to you tonight: the nation that went to the moon in peace for all mankind is ready to share its technology in peace with its nearest neighbors.

Tonight, I have discussed with you a new concept of partnership. I have made a commitment to action. I have given examples of actions we are prepared to take.

But as anyone familiar with government knows, commitment alone is not enough. There has to be the machinery to ensure an effective followthrough.

Therefore, I am also directing a major re-organization and upgrading of the U.S. Government structure for dealing with Western Hemisphere affairs.

As a key element of this, I have ordered preparation of a legislative request, which I shall submit to Congress, raising the rank of the Assistant Secretary of State for Inter-American Affairs to Under Secretary—thus giving the Hemisphere special representation. This new Under Secretary will be given authority to coordinate all U.S. Government activities in the Hemisphere.

Debates have long raged, both in the United States and elsewhere, over what our attitudes should be toward the various forms of government within the inter-American system.

Let me sum up my own views.

First, my own country lives by a democratic system which has preserved its form for nearly two centuries. We are proud of our system. We are jealous of our liberties. We hope that eventually most, perhaps even all, of the world's people will share what we consider to be the blessings of a genuine democracy.

We are aware that most people today, in most countries of the world, do not share those blessings.

I would be less than honest if I did not express my concern over examples of liberty compromised, of justice denied or of rights infringed.

Nevertheless, we recognize that enormous, sometimes explosive, forces for change are operating in Latin America. These create instabilities, and bring changes in governments. On the diplomatic level, we must deal realistically with governments in the inter-American system as they are. We have, of course, a preference for democratic procedures, and we hope that each government will help its people to move forward toward a better, a fuller and a freer life.

In this connection, however, I would stress one other point. We cannot have a peaceful community of nations if one nation sponsors armed subversion in another's territory. The Ninth Meeting of American Foreign Ministers clearly enunciated this principle. The "export" of revolution is an intervention which our system cannot condone, and a nation which seeks to practice it can hardly expect to share in the benefits of the community.

Finally, a word about what all this can mean for the world.

Today, the world's most fervent hope is for a lasting peace in which life is secure, progress is possible and freedom can flourish.

In each part of the world, we can have lasting peace and progress only if the nations directly concerned take the lead themselves in achieving it. And in no part of the world can there be a true partnership if one partner dictates its direction.

I can think of no assembly of nations better suited than ours to point the way in developing such a partnership. And a successfully progressing Western Hemisphere, demonstrating in action mutual help and mutual respect, will be an example for the world. Once again, by this example, we will stand for something larger than ourselves.

For three quarters of a century, many of us have been linked together in the Organization of American States and its predecessors in a joint quest for a better future. Eleven years ago, Operation Pan America was launched as a Brazilian initiative. More recently, we have joined in an Alliance for Progress, whose principles still guide us. Now our goal for the 70s should be a decade of Action for Progress for the Americas.

As we seek to forge a new partnership, we must recognize that we are a community of widely diverse people. Our cultures are different. Our perceptions are often different. Our emotional reactions are often different. Partnership—mutuality—these do not flow naturally. We have to work at them.

Understandably, perhaps, a feeling has arisen in many Latin American quarters that the United States "no longer cares."

My answer to that is simple.

We do care. I care. I have visited most of your countries. I have met most of your leaders. I have talked with your people. I have seen your great needs, as well as your great achievements.

And I know this, in my heart as well as in my mind: If peace and freedom are to endure in the world, there is no task more urgent than lifting up the hungry and the helpless, and putting flesh on the dreams of those who yearn for a better life.

Today, we share an historic opportunity.

As we look together down the closing decades of this century, we see tasks that summon the very best that is in us. But those tasks are difficult precisely because they do mean the difference between despair and fulfillment for most of the 600 million people who will live in Latin America by the year 2000. Those lives are our challenge. Those lives are our hope. And we could ask no prouder reward than to have our efforts crowned by peace, prosperity and dignity in the lives of those 600 million human beings, each so precious and each so unique—our children and our legacy.

Index

AFL-CIO, 62-63, 75
Agency for International Development (AID), 37, 75, 92
AIFLD Report, 63
Alessandri, Jorge, 39
Allende Gossens, Salvadore, 32, 36, 99, 101-102, 107
Alliance for Progress, 20, 32, 47, 72, 75, 97
  criticized, 48
  evaluated, 51, 53-54, 67
  funding, 48, 52, 53
  goals, 47-48
  obstacles, 52-53
American Institute for Free Labor Development (AIFLD), 62-63
Amiama Tió, Luis, 87, 88
Anti-Communism, U.S., 19, 20-21, 42, 73, 75, 76, 79, 94, 99, 103
Arbenz Guzmán, Jacobo, 79, 107
Argentina, 7, 100, 101
Aristy, Hector, 87
Arms control, 39-40, 69
Arosemena, Carlos, 45

Balaguer, Joaquin, 83, 84, 85, 91
Baldwin, Hanson, 38
Bay of Pigs invasion, 20, 72-73
Bennett, W. Tapley, Jr., 77, 86, 87, 91
Bentham, Jeremy, 61
Blaine, James G., 17
Bolivia, 58
  Chaco War, 57
  economy, 51, 52
  expropriation, 103
  1952 Revolution, 52
  population shift, 14
Bonnelly, Rafael, 91
Bosch, Juan, 58, 76, 80, 81, 82, 83, 84, 85, 86, 90, 91, 92
Brazil, 101
  1964 Revolution, 11-12
British Guiana, 74-76. *See also* Guyana
Bundy, McGeorge, 89
Bunker, Ellsworth, 89
Burnham, Forbes, 32, 75
Burr, Robert, 107
Byrnes, James F., 57

Caamaño Deño, Francisco, 86, 87, 90, 91-
   92
Cáceres Troncoso, Ramón, 83
Capitalism, 30
Cárdenas, Lázaro, 18
Castello Branco, Humberto, 45
Castillo Armas, Carlos, 79
Castro, Fidel, 30, 33-34, 44, 48, 52, 65,
   73, 75, 82, 102
Catholic Church, 11
Central Intelligence Agency (CIA),
   20, 30, 62, 72-73, 82,
   87, 89, 91, 100
Chile
   under Allende, 99-102
   Communists in, 32
   economy, 51
   expropriation, 99, 103
   reform, 13
Church, Frank, 42
Class factor, 11, 34-35
Cline, Howard, 105
Colombia
   economy, 51
   reform, 13
   and U.S. aid, 49, 52, 67
Colonialism, European, 16
Commercial Bureau of the American
   Republics, 17
Communism
   pluralism, 29-31
   U.S. attitude toward, 28-29, 36, 44,
      73, 87, 95-96, 97, 99-100
Communists
   ideological differences, 29-31
   in government, 31-32, 33, 34, 36, 78,
      101-102
Composite revolutions, 11-12
Connally, John, 59
Counterinsurgency, 42-43
Counterrevolutions, 11, 13
Crockett, Kennedy M., 91
Cuba
   acquired by U.S., 16
   Bay of Pigs, 20, 72-73, 103, 107
   Communism in, 33-34
   economy, 50-51, 52
   1962 missile crisis, 73-74
Czechoslovakia, 41

Debray, Régis, 34
Democracy, promoted by U.S., 18-19, 20,
   23, 27, 47, 66, 75, 78,
   94, 97, 107-108
"Democratizing" revolution, 11
Demonstrations, 9, 20, 94
Díaz, Porfirio, 56
Díaz Ordaz, Gustavo, 77
Dictatorships, 1, 45, 48, 51, 66, 92, 103,
   U.S. support for, 20, 23
Domínguez, Franklyn, 90
Dominican Republic, 56, 76, 81-86
   Center for Armed Forces Training
      (CEFA), 83
   economy, 50-51, 84
   1965 Civil War, 12, 51, 86-87
   U.S. intervention, 21, 51, 63, 87-92,
      103, 107
Dulles, John Foster, 19-20, 29, 64
Duvalier, François, 95, 103
Duvalier, Jean-Claude, 103

Economic assistance, 66-67, 98, 108
Economic development, 8, 47-48, 51-52,
   67
   collective action, 111
   by migration, 13-14
   personal income, 50
Economic interests, U.S., 15-16, 17, 20,
   109-111
   investment, 17, 18
   and national security, 18
   political considerations, 18-19, 20
   trade, 17, 109-110
Ecuador
   economy, 51
   literacy and voting, 11
   population shift, 13
Eisenhower, Dwight D., 47, 60, 95, 103,
   107
Eisenhower, Milton, 66
Encina, Dionisio, 30
England, 18, 32
Equality movement, 7
Evarts, William, 56
Export-Import Bank, 99, 102
Expropriation, 18, 20, 65, 96, 97, 98,
   99, 103, 109

Federal Bureau of Investigation (FBI), 89
Fiallo, Viriato, 82
Foreign Assistance Act, Hickenlooper
  Amendment, 98
Foreign Leader Exchange Program, 63
Foreign policy, U.S., 61-65, 91-92
  economic considerations, 15-16, 17,
    20, 96-97, 103, 109
  expansionism, 16
  ideological base, 20-21, 76, 94, 103, 111
  life of concepts, 2, 15
  recognition, 55-60
France, 41
Frondizi, Arturo, 84

García Godoy, Hector, 89-91
"Good government" revolt, 10-11
Good Neighbor Policy, 18, 56-57
Goulart, João, 11, 77
Government
  de facto, 56-57, 60
  reform, 7, 8, 13, 44
Grace Line Shipping, 62
Gran Colombia, 51
Guatemala, U.S. and, 20, 79, 103, 107
Guayaquil (Ecuador), 13
Guevara, Ernesto ("Che"), 34, 74
Guyana, 32

Haiti, 51, 103
Herter, Christian, 20
Hobbes, Thomas, 13
Honduras, 76
  population shift, 14
Hull, Cordell, 56
Huntington, Samuel P., 22

Illia, Arturo, 45
Imbert Barrera, Antonio, 88, 89
Inter-American Committee for the
  Alliance for Progress (CIAP), 97
International Monetary Fund, 84
International Petroleum Company,
  (IPC), 65, 98, 109
Interventionism, U.S., 18, 21, 26-27, 66,
  78, 80, 103, 105, 106, 107, 108
  Dominican Republic, 21, 51, 63, 87-92

Jagan, Cheddi, 32, 75
Jefferson, Thomas, 56, 58
Johnson, Lyndon B., 21, 47, 76, 89, 91,
  103, 107, 111
John XXIII, 82

Kaldor, Nicholas, 75
Kennedy, John F., 20, 47, 52, 73, 74, 75,
  76, 82, 93, 94, 103, 107
Khrushchev, Nikita, 34, 74
Kissinger, Henry, 93, 99-100

Land, availability, 6, 13-14
Latin America
  neglected by U.S., 19, 93
  pluralism, 1
  population growth, 6, 7, 14, 35, 50
Life expectancy, 51
Literacy, 6
Lombardo Toledano, Vicente, 30, 35

McCarthy, Joseph R., 29
Mann, Thomas, 77, 79, 80, 91, 105, 108
  Notre Dame speech, 78-79, 145 et seq.
Mao Tse-tung, 34
Marighela, Carlos, 35
Mexico
  Communists in, 30
  economy, 51, 52
  expropriation, 18
  population shift, 14
Migration, rural to urban areas, 6, 7
Military, Latin American, 37-38, 43-46, 97
  juntas by, 10, 41, 44-46, 76, 82, 86, 88,
    98
Military assistance, 38, 40-42, 68-69
Military power, U.S., 22, 26, 34
Mitchell, John N., 97
"Modernizing" revolution, 11
Molina Ureña, Rafael, 85, 86
Monroe Doctrine, 17
Morel Cerda, Manuel Ramón, 90
Moynihan, Daniel P., 93

National interests, U.S.
  economic aspects, 15-16, 17, 18, 20

ideological aspects, 20-21
political concerns, 18
territorial objectives, 16
vagueness of, 15
Nationalism, 62, 65, 94, 96
economic, 110
National security, Latin American, 38-39
National security, U.S., 21-23, 73, 106-107, 112
economic considerations, 18
and ideology, 23, 79
Nixon, Richard M., 21, 47, 66, 93, 94, 97, 103
Inter-American Press Association speech, 96-97, 155 *et seq.*
demonstration against, 20
Nuclear weapons, 68

Onganía, Juan Carlos, 45
Organization of American States (OAS), 60, 62, 89

"Palace Revolt," 10
Panama Canal Zone, n16
Paraguay: Chaco War, 57
economy, 51
Participatory politics, 7, 10, 35, 108
Partido Revolucionario Dominicano (PRD), 84, 87
Paz Estenssoro, Víctor, 77
Peguero, Belisario, 83
Pérez Jiménez, Marcos, 20, 64
Peru, 76
economy, 51
expropriation, 65, 98, 103, 109
military rule in, 41
Political organizations 7, 30, 34
Chilean, 101-102
Dominican Republic, 84, 86-87
Population
growth, 6, 7, 14, 35, 50
redistribution of, 13-14
rural, 6
See also Urban growth
Prado, Manuel, 39
Puerto Rico, acquired by U.S., 16, 26

Punta del Este, Charter of, 48
text, 127 *et seq.*

Quadros, Jânio, 84

Raborn, William, 77, 91
Recognition by U.S., 55-57
effect of, 57
non-recognition, 58-59
Reid Cabral, Donald, 83, 84, 85, 86
Repression, 12-13, 45, 108
Revolution
defined, 10
forms, 10
Rivera Cuesta, Marcos, 85
Rockefeller, Nelson, 42, 94, 95, 96, 99
Rockefeller Report, 23, 94, 95-98
Ronning, C. Neale, 56
Roosevelt, Franklin D., 18, 19, 23, 56
Roosevelt, Theodore, 18, 22, 78, 94, 107
Roosevelt Corollary, 17
Rusk, Dean, 75

San Pedro Sula (Honduras), 14
Santa Cruz (Bolivia), 14
Skinner, B.F., 61
Smith, Adam, 61
Socialism, 30-31, 65, 102
"Socializing" revolution, 11
Soviet Union
cooperation with U.S., 29
and Cuba, 34, 73-74, 100-101
missile crisis of 1962, 73-74
postwar policy, 27-28
Spanish-American War, 16, 27
Stalin, Josef, 28
Standard Oil Company of N.J., 62, 98
Stevenson, Adlai, 94
Stroessner, Alfredo, 77
Students, 45

Taft, William Howard, 17, 18, 78, 81, 107
Tito, Josip Broz, 28
Tobar Doctrine, 18
Torrijos, General, 45

Trujillo, Rafael, 12, 83, 87, 88
Trujillo, Ramfis, 83
Truman, Harry S., 19

United States
   and dictatorships, 20, 22
   diplomatic recognition by, 55-60
   neglect of Latin America, 19, 93
   pluralism, 2
   and revolutionary governments, 1-2, 14,
      63-64, 81
   and Soviet Union, 29
United States Information Agency, 64
Urban growth, 6, 7, 35
Uruguay: economy, 50
   voting in, 7

Valencia, Guillermo León, 49
Vaughn, Jack Hood, 77, 91
Velasco Ibarra, José Mariá, 84

Venezuela
   Communists in, 30
   dictatorship, 20
   economy, 51
   population shift, 13
   reform, 13
Viñas Román, Elby, 83
Violence, 9, 12
   representational, 9
   and repression, 12-13
Volman, Sacha, 82
Voting, 7, 11

Welles, Benjamin, 100
Wessín y Wessín, Elías, 83, 85, 86, 87, 90
Whitaker, Arthur, 105
Wilson, Woodrow, 18, 27, 78, 107
Wolfers, Arnold, 22
World War I, 27
World War II, 27, 38, 57